The
D-Day
Ships

The Union-Castle liner LLANGIBBY CASTLE served as an infantry landing ship during the Neptune operations. To land her troops, she carried 18 assault craft, some of which are seen suspended from davits while others are afloat in the foreground. [Imperial War Museum photograph]

THE D-DAY SHIPS

John de S. Winser

Neptune: the Greatest Amphibious Operation in History

HM cruiser MAURITIUS engaging shore targets on D-Day.

The Liberty ship
SAMAROVSK
loading army vehicles
in the London docks.
[IWM B5215]

© 1994 J. de S. Winser

Published by the World Ship Society,
28 Natland Road, Kendal LA9 7LT, England

ISBN 0 905617 75 4

CONTENTS

Total number of vessels listed - 5,015 (excluding the many hundreds of craft embarked in landing ships)

INDEX OF ALLIED NAMED VESSELS

ISLE OF GUERNSEY was one of the Red Ensign infantry landing ships: three of her six landing craft can be seen in this February 1944 photograph. [Southern Railway]

INTRODUCTION

A number of books have already been published on various aspects of the D-Day landings in Normandy: this is hardly surprising in view of the invasion's importance and the fact that its sheer scale made it unquestionably the greatest amphibious operation in history.

Gathered together here in one publication, probably for the first time, are listings of the naval and merchant ships which contributed to Operation Neptune's success during the month of June 1944. Whilst primarily concentrating on the ships, hence the title, the book does not neglect the vast number of landing and other craft which also played such a vital part.

The information has been researched from naval signals and from official plans, orders and reports compiled around the time of the operation. The study covers a period when, inevitably, some records are either incomplete or in conflict with each other: the work is, however, as accurate and comprehensive as I have been able to make it from the documents consulted. Data made available more recently has been shown *in italics*.

For their very substantial help to me in the preparation of this book, I am greatly indebted to Lieutenant-Commander Arnold Hague and to Mr Bob Todd (of the National Maritime Museum [NMM]). I would also like to express my sincere thanks to Messrs David Brown and Michael McAloon (both of the Naval Historical Branch) and to Mr Paul Kemp (of the Imperial War Museum [IWM]).

Whenever possible, in the selection of supporting illustrations, priority has been given to photographs taken around the time of Operation Neptune, the advantage of topicality taking precedence over quality in some instances. The reference numbers of prints from the IWM and NMM collections have been quoted, where known, to assist readers wishing to order prints from those museums.

As a schoolboy in London at the time, I was keenly aware of the events of that fateful month of June fifty years ago and offer this publication as my humble tribute to all who contributed to ensuring that Operation Neptune was such an historic success.

JOHN DE S. WINSER

OPERATION NEPTUNE

View from the Eastern Task Force flagship SCYLLA off the beach-head on D-Day, with the cruiser FROBISHER in the centre and the battleship WARSPITE to the right in the far distance. [IWM]

The Planning

Following the German occupation of France, Belgium and Holland in 1940, the inevitability had been accepted that it would require an assault across the English Channel to inflict a decisive defeat on Germany's armies in the west. This strategy had been formally agreed by Britain, the United States and their allies in April 1942. It remained the ultimate objective even though preliminary operations were carried out successfully to drive the enemy out of North Africa and to move allied forces, via Sicily, onto the Italian mainland, thereby freeing the Mediterranean for allied shipping.

On 5th August 1943, Prime Minister Winston Churchill embarked in the Southern Railway steamer MAID OF ORLEANS for the short passage down the Clyde to the liner QUEEN MARY waiting to take him to Canada for a meeting with President Roosevelt. It was fitting that MAID OF ORLEANS was destined to become one of the ships in the cross-Channel assault, the detailed plans for which were explained to Mr Churchill during his Atlantic crossing. The crucial decision was the selection of a landing area from the options available, extending from Holland in the east to Brittany in the west. The choice was finally made in favour of Normandy, where the beaches were suitable and protected from the prevailing winds, where the defences were less formidable and where the terrain was acceptable for airfield development and for the consolidation and subsequent expansion of the bridgehead. 'Overlord' was the codename assigned to the operation as a whole, with 'Neptune' being applied to the naval portion of it, involving the safe and timely arrival of the assault forces at their beaches, the cover of the landings and the support and build-up of the forces once ashore.

The problem of supplying the chosen beach-heads, where no major ports existed, was ultimately overcome by an ingenious plan to use prefabricated harbours brought from England and put together off the Normandy coast. A ring of five breakwaters (codenamed 'Gooseberries') would be formed by sinking, in shallow water, blockships (called 'Corncobs'), one of which would be the veteran French battleship COURBET, another the former British battleship CENTURION. An outer breakwater would be provided using floating steel tanks called 'Bombardons'. Within two of the five 'Gooseberries', harbours would be created each with an enclosed area some two miles in length and one mile in width. One of these artificial harbours, named 'Mulberries', was to be sited at St Laurent in the American landing area and was given the letter 'A' while the other - 'B' - was to be created off Arromanches to serve the British area. These harbours were later to be renamed St Laurent and Arromanches respectively.

The Preparations

Because of the immense task of ensuring that the allies would be sufficiently strong to undertake the assault, a preparation time of not less than nine months was required, in addition to the training and planning already undertaken. In Summer 1943, a target date of 1st May 1944 was set, although this was later postponed a month to enable extra landing craft to be built to expand the initial assault from three to five Army divisions. Seine Bay, the area of Normandy chosen for the assault, is some 50 miles across and stretches from Barfleur eastwards to the mouth of the Seine. Because it was ultimately intended that American forces should be supplied directly from the United States, their troops were assigned to the western sector, where their landing areas were named 'Utah' and 'Omaha', while the British 'Sword' and 'Gold' and the partially Canadian 'Juno' beaches were in the eastern sector. In May 1944, D-Day was set for the 5th of the following month, a time of favourable moon and tides, conditions which would still prevail on the 6th and 7th June but not thereafter. Naval units were required to be in their designated assembly positions by 29th May, a directive which involved shipping movements at almost every southern British port from the Mersey to Harwich as well as at Belfast and a number of Scottish locations.

From their diverse assembly areas, the complex plan called for all vessels of the invasion fleet to be funnelled into an approach corridor, the northern entrance to which would be marked by a buoy moored about twenty miles south of Hayling Island. Mine clearance ships would head the armada creating swept paths fifty miles southwards to the French coast, the corridors being indicated with flagged dan buoys each bearing a dim light to show the various shipping lanes during the night approach. The way would then be prepared for the assault ships and craft; for the supporting vessels and for the bombarding ships, due to operate up to twelve miles offshore but within range of each vessel's initially designated target.

The Distant Ships Set Out

Because of their slow speed, being old or damaged ships, the section of the 'Corncob' (blockship) fleet which had assembled in the estuary of the Forth set out as early as 23rd May on its journey through the Pentland Firth to Oban, escorted by the cruiser DURBAN which was herself to be scuttled or 'planted' off the French coast. Vastly expanded by the vessels which had assembled off Oban, the fleet then left on its slow southward journey through the Irish Sea. In order to confuse anyone reading into this convoy movement the start of the D-Day count-down, the ships' masters were led to believe that their destination was the Bristol Channel. They were however due to sail direct to the French coast and would have done so had bad weather not caused a 24-hour postponement to D-Day. Charts of Seine Bay had however been given to some tug skippers: when this error was realised, 'Immediate Top Secret' charts of the Boulogne area were quickly issued to counteract the earlier breach of security.

On 30th May, the first twenty-two coasters, which had loaded at Sharpness, Penarth, Port Talbot, Swansea, Avonmouth, Barry and Portishead, sailed from the Bristol Channel. Amongst them were four Norwegian vessels, EDLE, HEIEN, MARI and SKARV; the Dutch STARKENBORGH and ERNA, the

(Above) Full house in the run-up to D-Day at Southampton with landing craft (tank and headquarters) alongside in the New Docks. [IWM A23731]

(Below) In the foreground, DUKE OF WELLINGTON. Other infantry landing ships, in the background, are thought to be (left to right) MONOWAI, ISLE OF GUERNSEY, ST HELIER, BRIGADIER and BIARRITZ. [IWM]

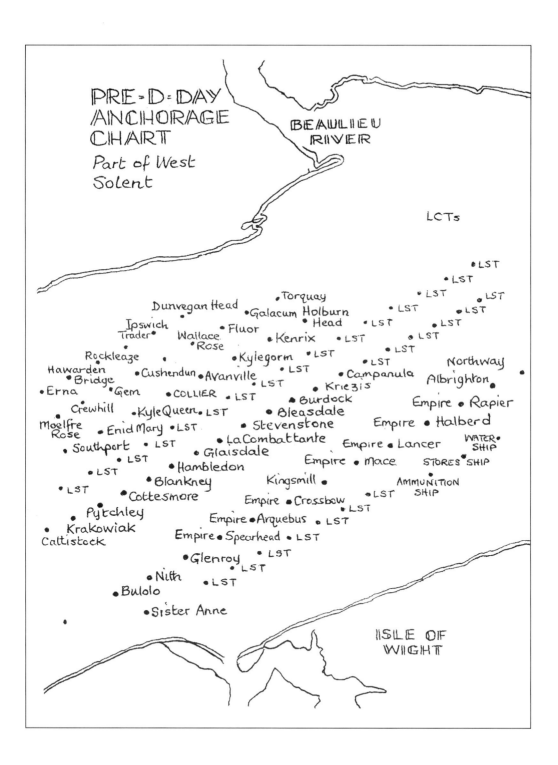

PRE-D-DAY
ANCHORAGE
CHART
Part of West
Solent

BEAULIEU
RIVER

LCTs

• LST
• LST
• LST   • LST
• LST   • LST
Torquay   • LST   • LST
Dunvegan Head   • Galacum Holburn   • LST   • LST
Ipswich   Head   • LST   • LST
Trader •   Wallace • Fluor   • Kenrix   • LST   • LST
Rockleaze •   • Rose   • Kylegorm   • LST
Hawarden •   • Cushendun • Avanville   • LST   Northway
• Bridge   • LST   • Campanula   Albrighton
• Erna   • Gem   • COLLIER • LST   • Kriezis
Crewhill   • Burdock   Empire • Rapier
Moelfre   • KyleQueen • LST   • Bleasdale
Rose   • Enid Mary • LST   • Stevenstone   Empire • Halberd
• Southport   • LST   • La Combattante   Empire • Lancer   WATER •
• LST   • Glaisdale   SHIP
• LST   • Hambledon   Empire • Mace   STORES SHIP
• LST   • Blankney   Kingsmill •   AMMUNITION
• LST   • Cottesmore   • LST   SHIP
Pytchley   Empire • Crossbow   • LST
• Krakowiak   Empire • Arquebus   • LST
Cattistock   Empire • Spearhead • LST
• Glenroy   • LST
• LST
• Nith   • LST
• Bulolo
• Sister Anne

ISLE OF
WIGHT

formerly French BIDASSOA and Robertson's CAMEO, FLUOR and GEM. They headed for the Solent, there to be joined from the opposite direction by thirty-three coasters including BROOMLANDS and SKELWITH FORCE, loaded with ammunition from Tilbury, and the Everard cased petrol carriers SEDULITY and SIGNALITY, which, in addition to their cargo of fuel, had loaded Royal Engineers' equipment and Bailey bridging in London's King George V Dock in mid-May: they were part of a fleet of no fewer than 126 coasters which had been waiting in the 20-mile stretch of the Thames between Blackwall and Tilbury. The last four ships named were destined to reach the beach-head on the evening of D-Day but, with the others, were in the meantime to wait in the western Solent. They took their places amongst over 500 ships in a vast anchorage, extending from Hurst Castle in the west to Bembridge in the east, in which every suitable space had been allocated for vessels assembling in the run-up to D-Day.

From their anchorages in the Clyde or Belfast Lough, the battleships of the bombarding fleet sailed on 2nd and 3rd June - HM Ships RAMILLIES and WARSPITE with the (British) Eastern Task Force and the USS ARKANSAS, TEXAS and, the Pearl Harbor survivor, NEVADA for the (American) Western. These five capital ships were escorted by British and US destroyers and accompanied by a formidable armada of cruisers, including MONTCALM and GEORGES LEYGUES, two 6-inch gun units of the French Navy. The 6-inch gun cruiser was regarded as ideal for medium range bombardment and the Eastern Task Force alone was equipped with sixty-two such guns on eight ships. As the bombardment ships moved southwards through the Irish Sea, overtaking the 'Corncobs' in the process, news was received of the postponement of D-Day so this fleet reversed course for twelve hours. Elsewhere vessels were recalled or ordered to delay their departure. The weather forecast for the 6th proved marginally better: the momentous operation was ordered to go ahead.

The Assault Armada Sails for France

Landing craft with the longest crossings set out early on the 5th. HMS SCYLLA, flagship of the Eastern Task Force, left Portsmouth Harbour at 1340 on the 5th as the first assault forces were passing through Spithead Gate. These included SIDMOUTH and the 9th Minesweeping Flotilla which, at 1915 that evening, started streaming their sweeps to clear the channels to the beach-heads. Minutes afterwards, the US minesweeper OSPREY sank, whilst under tow after sustaining mine damage. At about the same time, GLENROY and EMPIRE ARQUEBUS, part of the sizeable fleet of infantry landing ships (LSIs) left their West Solent anchorages for the British beaches. This 'Empire' vessel was one of thirteen American-built Red Ensign LSIs which had been transferred to the British Government under the Lend-Lease arrangement: they could carry up to twenty landing craft in which, after arriving off the French coast, their troops would make the final 7-11 mile dash between lowering position and shore. The US HQ ship ANCON left Plymouth so as to reach her assigned anchorage at Omaha: the forces under her command were destined to face some of the bloodiest fighting of the landings. Troops joining their Utah-bound LSIs at Tor Bay anchorage were ferried to their ships in landing craft from Torquay: troops embarking in Weymouth Bay, where over eighty ships were anchored, and Portland were similarly transported from Weymouth Quay.

The initial assault and follow-up ships had a lifting capability of nearly 160,000 troops and over 16,000 vehicles. The first of the bombarding ships opened fire soon after 0500 on 6th June: the US battleship TEXAS directed 250 rounds at six 6.2-inch gun emplacements at Pointe du Hoc. The heaviest bombardment took place during the first fifty minutes after the sun rose at 0558 that morning. The task was to silence, with saturating fire, not only the thirteen main coastal artillery batteries but also the beach defence forces and then, after the assault had gone in, to engage other targets assisted by ground and air spotters. Destroyers assisted the larger warships in these tasks. Naval action occurred early at the eastern extremity when three German torpedo boats on patrol, finding themselves unexpectedly confronted by an enemy fleet, fired and narrowly missed WARSPITE, RAMILLIES and the 'Sword' headquarters ship LARGS but hit the Norwegian destroyer SVENNER, twelve miles west of Le Havre. As the assault troops swept onto the shore and the battles developed, inevitably further naval casualties occurred. A delayed action mine took its toll of the US destroyer CORRY in the western

(Above) An aerial view taken over Lee-on-the-Solent on 5th June, 1944, looking towards the Isle of Wight. In the foreground is the tug anchorage, the large vessel to the right is their depot ship AORANGI and, just discernible in the middle distance, are tank landing ships and ADVENTURE and DESPATCH (in the centre) with (top left) PRINSES ASTRID and MAID OF ORLEANS. In the background are some of the roadway sections waiting to be towed to the Mulberry harbours. [IWM A23836]

Alongside at Southampton's Old Docks are the infantry landing ships DUKE OF ARGYLL (right) and ISLE OF GUERNSEY. [ABP]

sector while, just inside the northern limit of the eastern assault area, HM destroyer WRESTLER suffered a mine strike and had to be taken in tow.

One Assault Ship's Story

Edited extracts from the War History of the infantry landing ship MAID OF ORLEANS for early June 1944.

On 2nd June, MAID OF ORLEANS went alongside at Southampton to embark the troops who had been working with the ship and who had landed on 4th May. They were greeted as old friends by all on board. Great precautions were taken to ensure that unauthorised persons did not see the embarkation and all realised that the invasion day was not far distant. The ship returned to her Cowes anchorage where troops indulged in swimming and sunbathing. The ship was now sealed off and no communication with the shore was permitted.

The 4th June found a strong wind blowing with rough seas and, towards evening, all hands knew that D-Day was cancelled for the morrow. There was a general feeling of disappointment throughout the ship because of this: the weather was the main topic of conversation and interest. To the relief of everyone, orders were received that the ship would leave at 2100 that evening and the scene was like that of a school breaking up for the holidays, with singing and joking, writing of last letters home and the cleaning of weapons.

At 1900, Captain Payne made a short speech in which he told all hands what was expected of them and gave them an outline of the operations on the morrow and the ship's part in it. He was followed by Major Menday who explained the part his troops were to play. Having taken the first objectives - three machine gun nests on the beach, a strongpoint with walls 30ft thick and a gun battery, they were to go on across the river and canal, save the bridges and lock gates and defend these for three days, on their left flank would be the sea and, on their right, the paratroops who would be dropped that morning east of Caen.

The ship's position in the invasion force was to be on the extreme left (east), with the beach at Ouistreham as its objective. As protection, there would be a screen of cruisers, battleships and destroyers, whose task it was to hammer the shore batteries, particularly a six gun 16-inch battery, which the heavy bombers had failed to knock out the evening before. The troops on board comprised 16 officers and 247 other ranks and all, who could, turned in for some sleep: the troops in their hammocks slept as soundly as if bound for an exercise. At midnight, the Roman Catholic Chaplain handed over to the Purser the mail he had spent the evening censoring and remarked that every man had written in great spirits, telling their folks at home not to worry.

The ship weighed anchor at 2107 on 5th June, passing through the gate at 2158 and formed up single line ahead on HMS GLENEARN. Just as MAID OF ORLEANS was about to anchor on the far shore, a destroyer (SVENNER) blew up, having been hit amidships. She soon settled, the midship portion and funnel then disappeared as she broke in two and the bow and stern slowly came up in the form of a 'V'. Crew members were seen to be mustering on the fore-deck from which they dropped into the water, some to be picked up later: those who were below and in the engine room had no chance of escape.

At 0540, we anchored at the lowering position and at 0545 manned the craft. This proceeded in a most orderly manner, long practice having made each man familiar with his position in the different landing craft. As these were lowered at 0605, we of the ship's company silently sent them our good wishes for it will be remembered that these specially trained Commandos had been with us over a period of many months and had grown to become part of the ship's company. There was a heavy sea running at the time and so it was with a sigh of relief that the craft were seen safely away without mishap, each soldier wearing full kit and extra ammunition.

Opposite the place where our craft landed was an enemy stronghold and the beach was swept from end to end by machine gun and mortar fire. Many men never reached the beach and one craft had a

(Above) HM cruisers ARETHUSA (nearest), DANAE and MAURITIUS on 3rd June, 1944. [IWM A24094]

Bombarding Ships en route to Normandy

(Right) USS TEXAS (nearest) and, astern of her, HMS GLASGOW, USS ARKANSAS and the French cruiser GEORGES LEYGUES. [IWM A23923]

(Below) (right to left) HM ships DANAE, ARETHUSA and FROBISHER and the Polish DRAGON.

(Above) Assault ships of Force J1 led by (left to right) PRINCE HENRY, QUEEN EMMA, ULSTER MONARCH and INVICTA. [IWM A24344]

(Left) The 15-inch guns of HM battleship RAMILLIES lend their support to the bombardment of shore targets on D-Day. [IWM A23918]

(Below) The destroyer BEAGLE off the beach-head: three tank landing ships can be seen in the background. [IWM A23872]

(Above) Tank landing craft LCT 765 passes the infantry landing ship DUKE OF WELLINGTON: in the background a coaster and a Liberty ship.

(Right) The Liberty ship SAMBUT ablaze in the Strait of Dover on D-Day after being hit by long range gunfire. [NMM D755]

(Below) HM cruiser AJAX on 7th June, 1944. [IWM A23931]

(Above) A D-Day view off Juno of the infantry landing ships of Force J2 (left to right) MONOWAI, PRINCE DAVID, LADY OF MANN, ST HELIER, ISLE OF GUERNSEY, DUKE OF WELLINGTON, CLAN LAMONT and BRIGADIER. [IWM A23847]

(Right) Tank landing craft leaving their British anchorage. [IWM]

mortar bomb fall in the centre of it while packed with troops, killing two and wounding others. Although one air raid warning was sounded during the time the ship was anchored off the beaches, no enemy aircraft could have survived in a sky so dominated by our own aircraft. Five of our landing craft returned by 1030 and we were genuinely pleased to see them: one had struck a submerged obstruction and returned without any steering gear. The sixth craft had been lost by enemy action.

The weather was not good and, to hoist the landing craft, it was necessary to manoeuvre the ship with main engines to give them a lee, also to pour oil on the water to windward to assist them to get alongside. Most of the craft davits and lifting hooks were strained and damaged during this procedure. Whilst lying at anchor, heavy gunfire was experienced from shore batteries which appeared to be directed at us or at a convoy of tank landing ships which was passing close astern at the time. Having received a signal from GLENEARN to prepare to weigh anchor, the ship took her place in the return convoy when ordered to do so. MAID OF ORLEANS anchored in Cowes Roads at 2156 and so ended D-Day with every man of the ship's company happy to have taken part in this historic event. (End of extract.)

The Landings are Successful

After completing their initial task, the LSIs headed back to the UK to reload. The handling of such a large number of ships and craft in narrow and restricted waters presented a problem of considerable complexity and detailed timetables had to be followed in order to co-ordinate precisely all the many forces involved. There was little room for flexibility and, in fact, the initial convoys were generally punctual to within a few minutes. The Commanding Officer of the destroyer VIRAGO, in his report, said that 'the passage went without hitch and was a triumph for the organisation'. Over 150 sloops, escort destroyers, frigates, corvettes and other craft were allocated to accompany the assault and early convoys, with anti-submarine groups operating in the approaches to the Channel.

The only unexpected event was the completeness of tactical surprise. Enemy radar installations had been largely rendered ineffective by air action and the Germans had regarded the seas as being too rough on that day to permit an assault to be mounted. In any event, they had expected an attack at new moon, on a rising tide, in the neighbourhood of a good harbour and away from cliffs and dangerous shallow waters. In fact, the assault went in at low tide, when the moon was full, away from harbours and at some points below sheer cliffs. A daylight landing was made in order to increase the accuracy of air and naval bombardment and low tide was selected in order to expose the beach obstacles. Ship casualties were less than anticipated whereas casualties to landing and small craft proved higher than allowed for, although 75% of these were attributed to the weather. Diversionary activities were successfully conducted in the Strait of Dover to give the impression that another, or even the main, assault might be carried out in that area, thereby pinning down German forces unnecessarily.

The Build-up Convoys

The majority of over 300 large cargo vessels assigned to Neptune were of the American-built Liberty type, many of them carrying vehicles (mechanised transport) and their attendant troops. Early such arrivals in the American sector were HORACE GRAY from Newport, CHARLES WILLSON PEALE from Barry and EZRA WESTON from Cardiff. They approached the French coast on the morning of 7th June, simultaneously with eleven British-manned 'Sam' Liberty ships from the Thames which were serving the Eastern Task Force area. From a convoy of thirty-four Liberty ships en route southwards from the Clyde, four were to load at Falmouth, two at Plymouth and the remainder at Southampton. Loading in London's South West India Dock were OCEAN COURIER and Hain Line's TREVIDER; EMPIRE DEED was in Millwall Dock, MALAYAN PRINCE and FORT ESPERANCE in Royal Victoria and, at Berth 13, Royal Albert Dock, the Strick-managed EMPIRE STUART.

Detailed plans had been made for the routing of 362 coasters which were to help maintain a continuous flow of supplies to the beaches. Cargoes of ammunition for the British area were to be

(Above) The Polish Hunt class destroyer KRAKOWIAK, her guns trained on the French coast. [IWM A23898]

(Left) The infantry landing ship ST HELIER.

(Below) Mooring vessels position 'Bombardons' (200ft long floating steel tanks) off the French coast to form an outer breakwater. [IWM]

loaded aboard coasters at Southampton; at the Sussex ports of Littlehampton and Newhaven and also at Tilbury Dock and River Jetty. The loading of cased petrol was to be handled at London's King George V Dock, Poole, Southampton and Purfleet, while general stores were to be shipped at Grimsby, Southampton and, on the Thames, at Millwall, Tilbury and in the Royal Docks. In accordance with the plan, the first coaster convoy to return from the American beach-head included the Kelly-owned CREWHILL to load at Southampton; THE PRESIDENT to load ammunition at Fowey; SAINT RULE for Llanelly, CITRINE for Sharpness and LOTTIE R. for Port Talbot. HEIEN headed for Swansea and the Polish coasters, KATOWICE and KMICIC, for Penarth and Newport respectively. CLEMENT T. JAYNE was one of a number of vessels on bareboat charter from the United States and operated from Avonmouth direct to Utah.

It was not until about noon on D-Day that the operation's first merchant ship loss occurred and even then it happened over 100 miles from Normandy. The convoy of eleven 'Sam' ships, mentioned earlier, had set out from the Thames Estuary with one additional vessel in their midst. However, during the convoy's transit of the Strait of Dover, two shells from German batteries on the French coast set fire to the 7,000-ton Henderson-managed SAMBUT and she had to be abandoned. Astern of this convoy was another which included eight large troopships, with a gross tonnage of 88,000. These were the 16,000grt Anchor liner CAMERONIA; the Belgian LEOPOLDVILLE and Bibby's WORCESTERSHIRE and DEVONSHIRE, which, between them, had embarked over 9,000 servicemen at Tilbury Landing Stage. In the Thames Estuary they had been joined by the trooper LANCASHIRE; her fellow Bibby ship CHESHIRE; CITY OF CANTERBURY and the British India troopship NEURALIA, which had embarked their soldiers in London's King George V Dock. Despite the earlier sinking, this convoy ran the Channel gauntlet in broad daylight without a single shell being fired. Four of the ships were then required to wait off Portsmouth while the other four large troopships steamed on so as to reach the British assault area early on the 7th. Apparently due to an administrative error, it was not until the 11th that NEURALIA crossed to Gold.

SAMBUT's sinking had emphasised the vulnerability of shipping in the Dover strait and it was for this very reason that no major British ship had been routed that way for four years. Indeed, when WORCESTERSHIRE was required for Neptune service, she left Southampton for London not by the short route eastwards but by the long circuit via the north of Scotland. However, the Dover route now formed a vital link in the build-up plan for ships of all sizes: no subsequent convoy, however, came near to equalling the one just described, in terms of ship size. One of the next large convoys comprised twenty-nine vessels which had assembled in the Thames Estuary, including four assigned to serve as depot or repair vessels for the British area. They were the former French Chargeurs Reunis liner CAP TOURANE from Glasgow; Blue Funnel's ASCANIUS from Loch Ewe; the Belgian THYSVILLE from the Tyne and the former seaplane carrier HMS ALBATROSS. To repatriate casualties, hospital carriers were allocated: the sailing programme was however severely disrupted by the mining of both DINARD and ST JULIEN within just over an hour of each other on the evening of the 7th.

After disembarking their troops on D-Day, American personnel vessels were directed to West Country or Bristol Channel ports. The attack transport JOSEPH T. DICKMAN, formerly United States Lines' PRESIDENT ROOSEVELT, was back at Falmouth on the afternoon of the 7th. EXCHEQUER and MARINE RAVEN had reached the Omaha beaches on the morning of the 8th, having set out from South Wales in company with their Utah-bound consorts EXPLORER, BIENVILLE and EXCELSIOR. While en route to Normandy, this convoy had passed the returning BORINQUEN, GEORGE W. GOETHALS and GEORGE S. SIMONDS: these three were proceeding to Cardiff after disembarkation at Omaha. Not returning from France was the US trooper SUSAN B. ANTHONY: she had struck a mine while approaching the beach-head and had gone down but not until all personnel had been evacuated.

The Ancillary Ships and Craft

Over 1,500 craft and barges were required as ferries between the anchorage position of the larger ships and the shore. Ancillary operations included the laying of light buoys; the survey.of beach-head

(Above) Coastal forces' craft, a minesweeper and the infantry landing ships ISLE OF GUERNSEY and (in the far distance) DUKE OF WELLINGTON in the Eastern Task Force area. [IWM]

(Below) HM battleship RODNEY assists the bombarding fleet. [IWM A23960]

(Above) The hospital carrier DINARD under tow after striking a mine on 7th June, 1944.

(Right) HM destroyer SCOURGE at 30 knots while escorting KELVIN carrying Prime Minister Winston Churchill on 12th June, 1944. [IWM A24090]

(Below) The view outside Mulberry A with (on the left) some of the blockships including the former battleship CENTURION. [IWM]

(Left) Night scene at Sword during an air raid.

(Below) This aerial view of one of the beach-heads gives an idea of the intense activity: there are nearly 100 ships and craft within the area photographed. [IWM EA25992]

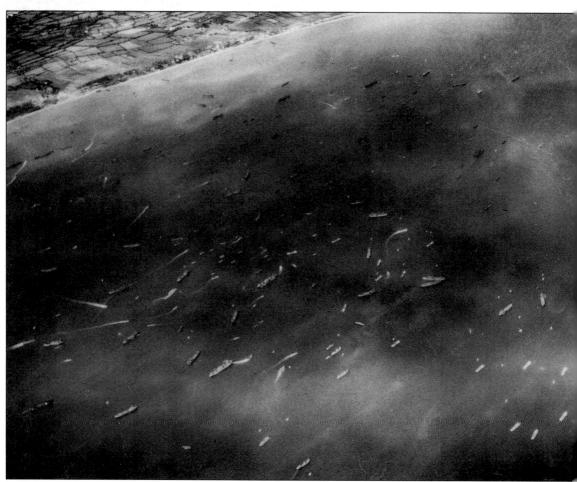

The northern entrance to Mulberry B (Arromanches) Harbour. [IWM]

areas; the provision of moorings; the production of defensive smoke screens and the repair of damaged vessels. There were about sixteen convoys and a similar number of landing craft groups at sea en route to or from the beaches at all times. The density of shipping movements brought its own hazards. Having been held in reserve, the battleship RODNEY left Spithead Gate at 0300 on the 7th, escorted by the cruiser SIRIUS, destroyer BLEASDALE and frigate RIOU, and shortly afterwards rammed the tank landing craft LCT 427, which sank with all hands. The battleship continued to Sword to join the bombardment fleet until the 9th: her sister, NELSON, reached the British area on the 11th but RODNEY's return to French waters was delayed when stocks of 16-inch high explosive ammunition fell to a mere 125 rounds.

Surviving the Great Storm

In the great 4-day Channel storm which started on 19th June - the worst during any June for forty years - the Hughes coaster WALLACE ROSE lost both anchors but her skipper skilfully kept her under way off the coast for a couple of days so that her cargo could be discharged as soon as the gale slackened. The storm left 800 craft stranded on the beaches and wrecked Mulberry A. The repercussions of an operational failure, due to bad weather or enemy action, would have been too hideous to contemplate for the allies. In the event, it was a complete success, involving hundreds of thousands of men and women of all services and the co-ordination of thousands of ship and craft movements. The Sword beach-head closed on 29th June and Operation Neptune officially ended on 30th June in the British sector and on 3rd July in the American: nevertheless the shuttle service of men and supplies continued unabated. By these dates, ships had conveyed to France more than 800,000 personnel; in excess of 130,000 vehicles and at least 400,000 tons of stores. In the words of Neptune's commander-in-chief - Admiral Sir Bertram Ramsay - it was 'the greatest amphibious operation in history'. Without doubt, so it will remain, for all time.

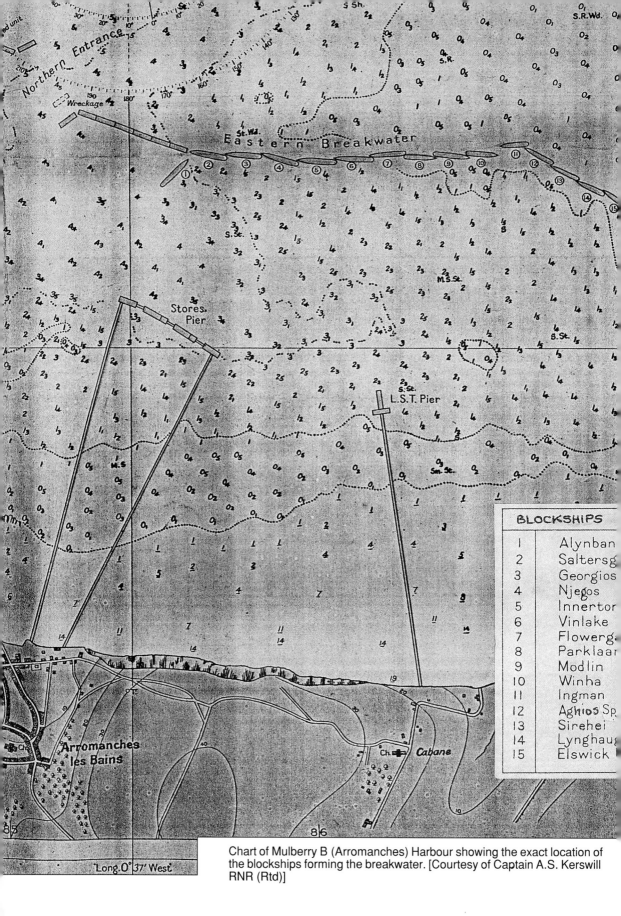

BLOCKSHIPS

1	Alynban
2	Saltersg
3	Georgios
4	Njegos
5	Innertor
6	Vinlake
7	Flowerg
8	Parklaar
9	Modlin
10	Winha
11	Ingman
12	Aghios Sp
13	Sirehei
14	Lynghau
15	Elswick

Chart of Mulberry B (Arromanches) Harbour showing the exact location of the blockships forming the breakwater. [Courtesy of Captain A.S. Kerswill RNR (Rtd)]

The Bombardment of Cherbourg on 25th June, 1944. (Above) The view ahead from HM cruiser ENTERPRISE en route to Cherbourg. The cruiser to the left is USS QUINCY and, to the right, HMS GLASGOW, with the battleship USS NEVADA in centre distance. [IWM A24300] (Below) The US battleship TEXAS coming under enemy fire.

BRIEF CHRONOLOGY

Date	Main events	Allied ships lost and some of those incapacitated. Details given in section indicated after vessel's name
1944 **May**		
23rd	First Corncobs left the Forth for Oban and Normandy	
29th	Naval units required to be in their designated assembly areas	
30th	First coasters left the Bristol Channel for the Solent then Normandy	
June		
2nd/ 3rd	Bombarding ships left the Clyde and Belfast	
4th	Midget submarines X20 and X23 positioned off Normandy coast as navigational beacons. D-Day postponed 24 hours until 6th owing to bad weather: assault craft already en route recalled, bombarding ships reversed course for 12 hours and Corncobs ordered to Poole Bay	
5th	Assault ships left for Normandy. Minesweeping operations started	OSPREY [B6]
6th	D-Day. Bombarding and assault forces arrived Seine Bay. Initial forces landed at dawn. First Mulberry tows left Portland	CORRY [B3], SAMBUT [A2], SVENNER [B3], WRESTLER [B3]
7th	First Corncob planted. First build-up convoys arrived	DINARD [C7], ST JULIEN [C7], SUSAN B. ANTHONY [A1], TIDE [B6]
8th		CHANT 61 [C13], GLENNON [B3], LAWFORD [B1], LST 499 [A4], MEREDITH [B3], MINSTER [C8], RICH [B4]
9th		LST 314 [A4], LST 376 [A4], MEREDITH [B3], ULSTER [B3]
10th	First coaster unloaded at Mulberry B	ASHANTI [A3], BRACKENFIELD [A3], CHARLES MORGAN [A2], DUNGRANGE [A3], GLENNON [B3], TEME [B5]
11th	All Gooseberries completed, two being expanded into Mulberries A and B	HALSTED [B4], LST 496 [A4], PARTRIDGE [C15], SESAME [C15]
12th		BRITISH ENGINEER [C13], NELSON (USS) [B3]
13th		BOADICEA [B3], MONARCH [C4], REIAS [A3]

The infantry landing ship EMPIRE LANCE with landing craft in May 1944. [IWM A23095]

14th		CHANT 69 [C13]
15th		BLACKWOOD [B5], MOURNE [B5]
16th		ALERT [C3], BLACKWOOD [B5]
17th		GLENROY [A1]
18th		ALBERT C. FIELD [A3]
19th	Mulberries 90% complete and handling 2,000 tons per day. Gale started to disrupt convoys and prevent unloading	CHANT 7 [C13], LST 523 [A4]
20th	Gale continued	ASA ELDRIDGE [A3], CHANT 23 [C13], LA SURPRISE [B4], RONDO [A3], SOLITAIRE [C15], WESTDALE [A3]
21st	Gale continued	DAVIS [B3], FURY [B3], THE PRESIDENT [A3]
22nd	Gale abated: unloading restarted	DUNVEGAN HEAD [A3], KYLEGORM [A3]
23rd		DUNDAS [C15], GLAISDALE [B3], NESTTUN [A3], PERSIAN [B6], SCYLLA [B1]
24th		DERRYCUNIHY [A2], EMPIRE LOUGH [A3], FENTONIAN [C14], FORT NORFOLK [A2], GURDEN GATES [A3], LORD AUSTIN [B4], SWIFT [B3]
25th	Bombardment of Cherbourg	GOODSON [B5]
26th	Mulberry A abandoned following gale damage	
27th		PINK [B4], STELLA RIGEL [B6]
28th		CHARLES W. ELIOT [A2], MAID OF ORLEANS [A1]
29th		EMPIRE PORTIA [A2], H.G. BLASDEL [A2], JAMES A. FARRELL [A2], JOHN A. TREUTLEN [A2]
30th	Operation Neptune ended in British sector	
July		
2nd		EMPIRE BROADSWORD [A1]
3rd	Operation Neptune ended in US sector	

SOME EXPLANATORY NOTES

1) Abbreviations in regular use (where not explained in the section heading)

Br   -   British

dwt   -   deadweight tonnage

ETA   -   expected time of arrival

HM   -   His Majesty's (British Royal Navy)

HQ   -   headquarters

MoWT -   (British) Ministry of War Transport

US   -   United States

The assault convoys were generally given a letter (indicating their beach-head destination) and a number (denoting their sailing sequence). Subsequent convoys were allocated codes to show country of departure, UK assembly area, type of vessel of which they were mainly composed, a number showing their sailing sequence and, when a convoy was in more than one part, a further designator. For instance, Convoy ETC2Y meant -

E =   **E**ngland (as opposed to **F**rance on the return convoy)

T =   **T**hames (as opposed to **B** [**B**ristol Channel], **C** [**C**ornwall and Devon], **P** [**P**ortland], **W** [Isle of **W**ight/Solent area] and **X** [Newhaven, Susse**x**])

C =   **C**oasters (as opposed to **L** [**L**anding Ships, Tank], **M** [**M**echanised Transport ships] or **P** [**P**ersonnel])

2 =   2nd convoy of that type

Y =   **W, X, Y** and **Z** were suffixes to indicate that a convoy was divided into two or more parts (**W** means the Isle of **W**ight/Solent portion of a divided convoy).

This coding system has been quoted alongside most of the ship listings in this book.

2) Where it is required to show that a ship was on loan from another country, that country has been included in the listing [eg 'Br (MoWT) US' indicating a British ship on loan or bareboat charter from the United States].

3) When no sailing confirmation has been traced in the official records (or, as sometimes, when no sailing signal was ever sent), the planned convoy movement has been shown with the prefix 'intended for'.

4) The term 'Solent' in this publication includes Spithead, Cowes, St Helens and Southampton Water; 'Portland' includes anchorages in Weymouth Bay; 'Thames' indicates the Thames Estuary off Southend and 'London' includes Tilbury.

5) Tonnage given for merchant ships is gross registered.

Assault Force J1. [IWM]

SHIPS AND CRAFT LISTED BY TYPE

PART A
THE VESSELS WHICH CARRIED THE SOLDIERS, THEIR VEHICLES, STORES AND EQUIPMENT

Section A1 - INFANTRY ASSAULT SHIPS, TROOPSHIPS AND ATTACK TRANSPORTS

including British and Canadian infantry landing ships (LSI) [large (L), medium (M), small (S) and hand-hoisting (H)] and US attack transports (APA), attack cargo ships (AKA) and transports (XAP).

The infantry assault ships, attack transports and craft were entrusted with carrying the initial waves of fighting soldiers to the D-Day assault areas. On completion of this task, they returned and joined the troopships in bringing across the Channel the reinforcement troops. Ranging from 16,000-ton converted passenger liners down to cross-Channel steamers one tenth of that size, these ships converged on Normandy from South Wales, the West Country, Weymouth Bay, the Solent and the Thames Estuary. A number of the vessels which took part in the initial landings remained to operate the cross-Channel troop shuttle, a service which continued for the remainder of the European war and beyond.

NAME OF VESSEL   Tonnage/year of build, nationality (owner), type - origin and/or assembly area, destination and convoy of first sailing: other information. (All dates are June 1944 unless otherwise stated.)

ACHERNAR   6,200/44   US AKA - left Avonmouth 24th May, embarkation at Plymouth, left Plymouth Sound anchorage, arrived Omaha 6th (Follow-up Convoy B2F) carrying US Army HQ: left Omaha 11th: at Swansea 20th

AMSTERDAM   4,220/30   Br (London & North Eastern Railway) cross-Channel passenger vessel as LSI(H) (capacity 420 troops: carried 6 landing craft) - embarkation at anchorage from landing craft from Weymouth, left Weymouth Bay (Anchorage G7) 5th, arrived Omaha 6th (Force J4[O4]) (Assault Convoy O1): in the Clyde 12th for conversion to hospital carrier

ANNE ARUNDEL   7,796/41   US (Moore-McCormack) vessel as XAP (capacity 2,124 troops: carried 24 landing craft) - embarkation at anchorage from landing craft from Weymouth, left Portland Harbour (Anchorage CC4) 5th, arrived Omaha 6th (Force O3) (Assault Convoy O1)

BARNETT   7,712/28   US (Grace) passenger/cargo liner SANTA MARIA as APA (capacity 1,295 troops) - ex Falmouth, embarkation at Tor Bay anchorage from landing craft from Torquay, left Tor Bay 5th, arrived Utah 6th (Force U) (Assault Convoy U1A): returned, via Weymouth Bay to land casualties, to Falmouth

BEN-MY-CHREE   2,586/27   Br (Isle of Man Steam Packet) cross-Channel passenger vessel as LSI(H) (capacity 428 troops: carried 6 landing craft) - embarkation at anchorage from landing craft from Weymouth, left Weymouth Bay (Anchorage G5) 5th, arrived Omaha 6th (Force J4[O4]) (Assault Convoy O1): returned to Southampton for repairs

BIARRITZ 2,388/15 Br (Southern Railway) cross-Channel passenger vessel as LSI(H) (capacity 407 troops and 6 landing craft) (Force J2 reserve LSI) - ex Solent (Anchorage 7/2), arrived Eastern Task Force area 8th (Convoy EWP1): left 2000 8th

BIENVILLE 6,165/43 US (Waterman) vessel as troopship (capacity 1,850 troops) - embarkation at Cardiff, left Bristol Channel 2115 6th, ETA Utah 8th (Convoy EBP2)

BORINQUEN 7,114/31 US (Agwilines) vessel as troopship (capacity 1,450 troops) - embarkation at Swansea, left Bristol Channel 5th, arrived Omaha 0830 7th (Convoy EBP1/B3): left 2140 7th for Cardiff (ETA 9th)

BRIGADIER 2,294/28 Br (Southern Railway) cross-Channel passenger vessel WORTHING as HM LSI(H) (carried 6 landing craft) - embarkation at Southampton (Berth 37), left Solent (Anchorage 18/3) 5th, arrived Juno 6th (Force J2) (Assault Convoy J10): returned to Solent where arrived 2310 6th: left for Newhaven 10th

CAMERONIA 16,297/20 Br (Anchor) passenger liner as troopship - after embarking about 2,680 troops at London (Tilbury Landing Stage) 1207-1427 4th, left 1427 4th, left Thames 6th, left Solent 7th, arrived Gold 8th (Convoy EWP1): left 2000 8th, in the Clyde 15th

CANTERBURY 2,910/29 Br (Southern Railway) cross-Channel passenger vessel as LSI(H) (capacity 436 troops: carried 6 landing craft) - embarkation at Southampton (Berth 37), left Solent (Anchorage 22/c3) 5th, arrived Juno 6th (Force J1) (Assault Convoy J9): returned to Weymouth Bay where arrived 7th

CHARLES CARROLL 8,100/42 US APA (capacity 1,402 troops: carried 31 landing craft) - embarkation at anchorage from landing craft from Weymouth, left Portland Harbour (Anchorage CC2) 5th, arrived Omaha 6th (Force O2) (Assault Convoy O1): returned to Portland where arrived 7th

CHESHIRE 10,552/27 Br (Bibby) passenger/cargo liner as troopship (capacity 2,200 troops) - embarkation at London (King George V Dock), left Thames 6th, arrived Juno 0930 7th (Convoy ETP1)

CITY OF CANTERBURY 8,331/22 Br (City) passenger/cargo liner as troopship (capacity 1,519 troops) - embarkation at London (King George V Dock), left Thames 6th, arrived Gold 0930 7th (Convoy ETP1)

CLAN LAMONT 7,526/39 Br (Clan) vessel as LSI(L) (capacity 1,285 troops: carried 18 landing craft) - embarkation at Southampton (Berth 40), left Solent (Anchorage 18/5) 5th, arrived Juno 6th (Force J2) (Assault Convoy J10): returned to Southampton: slightly damaged in collision 7th

BORINQUEN in February 1945. [NMM P21627]

DEVONSHIRE 11,275/39 Br (Bibby) troopship - embarked about 1,970 troops at London (Tilbury Landing Stage) 4th, left Thames 6th, arrived Juno 0930 7th (Convoy ETP1)

DOROTHEA L. DIX 6,736/40 US (American Export) vessel EXEMPLAR as XAP (capacity 1,550 troops: carried 24 landing craft) - embarkation at anchorage from landing craft from Weymouth, left Portland Harbour (Anchorage DD3) 5th, arrived Omaha 6th (Force O3) (Assault Convoy O1): returned to Portland where arrived 7th

DUKE OF ARGYLL 3,814/28 Br (London Midland & Scottish Railway) cross-Channel passenger vessel as LSI(H) (capacity 482 troops: carried 6 landing craft) - embarkation at Southampton (Berth 37), left Solent (Anchorage 22/b4) 5th, arrived Juno 6th (Force J1) (Assault Convoy J9): returned to Solent: ordered to Glasgow for conversion to hospital carrier 8th

DUKE OF WELLINGTON 3,743/35 Br (London Midland & Scottish Railway) cross-Channel passenger vessel DUKE OF YORK as HM LSI(H) (carried 6 landing craft) - embarkation at Southampton (Berth 38), left Solent (Anchorage 7/4) 5th, arrived Juno 6th (Force J2) (Assault Convoy J10): returned to Solent

EMPIRE ANVIL 7,177/44 Br (MoWT) US LSI(L) (capacity 1,310 troops: carried 20 landing craft) - embarkation at anchorage from landing craft from Weymouth: left Portland Harbour (Anchorage CC5) 5th, arrived Omaha 6th (Force O1) (Assault Convoy O1)

EMPIRE ARQUEBUS 7,177/44 Br (MoWT) US LSI(L) (capacity 1,310 troops: carried 18 landing craft) - embarkation at Southampton (Old Docks), left Solent (Anchorage 5/a5) 1830 5th, arrived Gold 6th (Force G1) (Assault Convoy G9B)

EMPIRE BATTLEAXE 7,177/43 Br (MoWT) US LSI(L) (capacity 1,195 troops: carried 18 landing craft) - embarkation at anchorage from paddle steamers MERSTONE and SHANKLIN from Portsmouth Harbour 3rd, left Solent (Anchorage 25/2) 5th, arrived Sword 0533 6th (Force S3) (Assault Convoy S7)

EMPIRE BROADSWORD 7,177/43 Br (MoWT) US LSI(L) (capacity 1,310 troops: carried 18 landing craft) - embarkation at anchorage from paddle steamers MERSTONE and SHANKLIN from Portsmouth Harbour 3rd, left Solent (Anchorage 25/1) 5th, arrived Sword 0533 6th (Force S3) (Assault Convoy S7): on a subsequent voyage, mined while en route from Omaha, turned over to starboard and sank 1835 2nd July.

DUKE OF ARGYLL [IWM]

EMPIRE HALBERD [IWM A23103]

EMPIRE CROSSBOW 7,177/44 Br (MoWT) US LSI(L) (capacity 1,310 troops: carried 18 landing craft) - embarkation at Southampton (Berth 38), left Solent (Anchorage 5/a6) 1830 5th, arrived Gold 6th (Force G1) (Assault Convoy G9B)

EMPIRE CUTLASS 7,177/43 Br (MoWT) US LSI(L) (capacity 1,310 troops: carried 18 landing craft) - embarkation at anchorage from paddle steamers MERSTONE and SHANKLIN from Portsmouth Harbour 3rd, left Solent (Anchorage 25/3) 5th, arrived Sword 0533 6th (Force S3) (Assault Convoy S7)

EMPIRE GAUNTLET 7,177/44 Br (MoWT) US LSI(L) (capacity 1,310 troops: carried 20 landing craft) - ex Falmouth, embarkation at Tor Bay anchorage from landing craft from Torquay, left Tor Bay anchorage 5th, arrived Utah 6th (Force U) (Assault Convoy U1A): returned, via Weymouth Bay where arrived 7th, to Plymouth

EMPIRE HALBERD 7,177/43 Br (MoWT) US LSI(L) (capacity 1,310 troops: carried 18 landing craft) - embarkation at Southampton (Old Docks), left Solent (Anchorage 5/a10) 5th, arrived Gold 6th (Force G2) (Assault Convoy G10B)

EMPIRE JAVELIN 7,177/44 Br (MoWT) US LSI(L) (capacity 1,310 troops: carried 20 landing craft) - embarkation at anchorage from landing craft from Weymouth, left Portland Harbour (Anchorage DD1) 5th, arrived Omaha 6th (Force O2) (Assault Convoy O1)

EMPIRE LANCE 7,177/43 Br (MoWT) US LSI(L) (capacity 1,310 troops: carried 18 landing craft) - embarkation at Southampton (Old Docks), left Solent (Anchorage 5/a9) 5th, arrived Gold 6th (Force G2) (Assault Convoy G10B): left 1530 6th for Solent where arrived 0230 7th

EMPIRE MACE 7,177/43 Br (MoWT) US LSI(L) (capacity 1,310 troops: carried 18 landing craft) - embarkation at Southampton (Old Docks), left Solent (Anchorage 5/a8) 5th, arrived Gold 6th (Force G2) (Assault Convoy G10B)

EMPIRE RAPIER 7,177/43 Br (MoWT) US LSI(L) (capacity 1,310 troops: carried 18 landing craft) - embarkation at Southampton (Old Docks), left Solent (Anchorage 5/a11) 5th, arrived Gold 6th (Force G2) (Assault Convoy G10B)

EMPIRE SPEARHEAD 7,177/44 Br (MoWT) US LSI(L) (capacity 1,310 troops: carried 18 landing craft) - embarkation at Southampton (Old Docks), left Solent (Anchorage 5/a4) 1830 5th, arrived Gold 6th (Force G1) (Assault Convoy G9B)

EXCELSIOR 6,685/43 US (American Export) vessel as troopship (capacity 2,590 troops) - embarkation at Newport, left Bristol Channel 2115 6th, ETA Utah 8th (Convoy EBP2)

EXCHEQUER 6,683/43 US (American Export) vessel as troopship (capacity 2,216 troops) - embarkation at Swansea, left Bristol Channel 2115 6th, ETA Omaha 8th (Convoy EBP2): returned to Swansea (ETA 11th)

EXPLORER 6,736/39 US (American Export) vessel as troopship (capacity 2,198 troops) - embarkation at Cardiff, left Bristol Channel 2115 6th, ETA Utah 8th (Convoy EBP2)

GEORGE S. SIMONDS 8,357/15 US vessel H.F. ALEXANDER as troopship (capacity 1,936 troops) (replacing CRISTOBAL) - embarkation at Swansea, left Bristol Channel 5th, arrived Omaha 0830 7th (Convoy EBP1/B3): left 2140 7th for Cardiff (ETA 9th)

GEORGE W. GOETHALS 12,093/42 US troopship (capacity 1,976 troops) - embarkation at Swansea, left Bristol Channel 5th, arrived Omaha 0830 7th (Convoy EBP1/B3): left 2140 7th for Cardiff (ETA 9th)

GLENEARN 9,784/38 Br (Glen) cargo liner as HM LSI(L) (capacity 1,089 troops: carried 24 landing craft) - embarkation at anchorage from paddle steamers MERSTONE and SHANKLIN from Portsmouth Harbour 3rd, left Solent (Anchorage 25/4) 2145 5th, arrived Sword 0533 6th (Force S3) (Assault Convoy S7)

GLENROY 9,809/38 Br (Glen) cargo liner as HM LSI(L) (capacity 1,098 troops: carried 24 landing craft) - embarkation at Southampton (Old Docks), left Solent (Anchorage 5/a3) 1830 5th, arrived Gold 6th (Force G1) (Assault Convoy G9B): left 1530 6th for Solent where arrived 0230 7th: on a subsequent voyage, engine room flooded by acoustic mine explosion while leaving Utah 1720 17th, left Omaha in tow of tug KIOWA 0845 18th, en route tow taken over by ZWARTE ZEE which arrived Solent 2400 18th then continued to Southampton where arrived 0845 20th

HENRICO 7,800/43 US APA (capacity 1,622 troops: carried 27 landing craft) - embarkation at anchorage from landing craft from Weymouth, left Portland Harbour (Anchorage DD4) 5th, arrived Omaha 6th (Force O1) (Assault Convoy O1): returned to Portland where arrived 7th

INVICTA 4,178/40 Br (Southern Railway) cross-Channel passenger vessel as HM LSI(H) (capacity 450 troops: carried 6 landing craft) - embarkation at Southampton (Berth 37), left Solent (Anchorage 22/b1) 5th, arrived Juno 6th (Force J1) (Assault Convoy J9): returned to Solent

ISLE OF GUERNSEY 2,143/30 Br (Southern Railway) cross-Channel passenger vessel as LSI(H) (capacity 383 troops: carried 6 landing craft) - embarkation at Southampton (Berth 38), left Solent (Anchorage 7/3) 5th, arrived Juno 6th (Force J2) (Assault Convoy J10): returned to Solent 6th then to Newhaven where arrived 9th

ISLE OF THANET 2,701/25 Br (Southern Railway) cross-Channel passenger vessel as LSI(H) and reserve HQ ship if HILARY and ROYAL ULSTERMAN became casualties (capacity 424 troops: carried 6 landing craft) - embarkation at Southampton (Berth 38), left Solent (Anchorage 22/b2) 5th, arrived Juno 6th (Force J1) (Assault Convoy J9): returned to Solent 6th: became ferry control HQ ship at Gold 30th (replacing ALBRIGHTON)

JOSEPH T. DICKMAN 13,858/22 US passenger liner PRESIDENT ROOSEVELT as APA (capacity 2,050 troops) - ex Falmouth, embarkation at Tor Bay anchorage from landing craft from Torquay, left Tor Bay anchorage 5th, arrived Utah 0240 6th (Force U) (Assault Convoy U1A): returned, via Weymouth Bay where arrived 7th to land casualties, to Falmouth where arrived 1517 7th

LADY OF MANN 3,104/30 Br (Isle of Man Steam Packet) cross-Channel passenger vessel as LSI(H) (capacity 490 troops: carried 6 landing craft) - embarkation at Southampton (Berth 39), left Solent (Anchorage 18/1) 5th, arrived Juno 6th (Force J2) (Assault Convoy J10): returned to Weymouth Bay where arrived 7th

LANCASHIRE on 23rd May, 1944. [NMM P23184]

LAIRDS ISLE   1,783/11   Br (Burns & Laird) cross-Channel passenger vessel as LSI(H) (carried 6 landing craft) - embarkation at Southampton (Berth 40), left Solent (Anchorage 22/c4) 5th, arrived Juno 6th (Force J1) (Assault Convoy J9): returned to Solent then Newhaven where arrived 9th

LANCASHIRE   9,557/17   Br (Bibby) troopship (capacity 2,035 troops) - embarkation at London (King George V Dock), left Thames 6th, arrived Juno 0930 7th (Convoy ETP1)

LEOPOLDVILLE   11,509/29   Belgian (Maritime Belge) passenger/cargo liner as troopship - after embarking about 2,110 troops at London (Tilbury Landing Stage) 0630-0930 4th, left at 0955 4th, left Thames 6th, left Solent 7th, arrived Gold 8th (Convoy EWP1): left 2000 8th: damaged in collision with LST 28 25th

LLANGIBBY CASTLE   11,951/29   Br (Union-Castle) passenger liner as LSI(L) (capacity 1,644 troops: carried 18 landing craft) - embarkation at Southampton (Berth 39), left Solent (Anchorage 18/8) 5th, arrived Juno 6th (Force J1) (Assault Convoy J9): returned to Solent

LONGFORD   1,913/06   Br (British & Irish) cross-Channel passenger vessel as troopship - left Clyde 16th, via Solent: after embarkation, left Newhaven 24th, ETA Juno 25th (Convoy EXP15)

LOUTH   1,915/06   Br (British & Irish) cross-Channel passenger vessel as troopship - left Clyde 16th: after embarkation, left Newhaven 21st, ETA Gold 23rd (Convoy EXP13W)

MAID OF ORLEANS   2,386/18   Br (Southern Railway) cross-Channel passenger vessel as LSI(H) (capacity 448 troops: carried 6 landing craft) - embarkation at Southampton (Berth 39), left Solent (Anchorage 22/b13) 2107 5th, arrived Sword 0540 6th (Force J4) (Assault Convoy S7): returned to Solent where arrived 2156 6th; on a subsequent voyage, sunk by U-boat *[U-988]* torpedo 2320 28th while returning to Solent

MARINE RAVEN   11,757/43   US troopship (capacity 2,546 troops) (replacing MARINE ROBIN) - embarkation at Swansea, left Bristol Channel 2115 6th, ETA Omaha 8th (Convoy EBP2): returned to Swansea (ETA 11th)

MECKLENBURG   2,907/22   Dutch (Zeeland) cross-Channel passenger vessel as LSI(H) (capacity 344 troops: carried 6 landing craft) - embarkation at Southampton (Berth 39), left Solent (Anchorage 22/b3) 5th, arrived Juno 6th (Force J1) (Assault Convoy J9): returned to Solent

MONOWAI   10,852/25   New Zealand (Union) passenger/cargo liner as LSI(L) (capacity 1,308 troops: carried 19 landing craft) - embarkation at Southampton (Berth 38), left Solent (Anchorage 18/4) 5th, arrived Juno 6th (Force J2) (Assault Convoy J10): returned to Solent

NEURALIA   9,182/12   Br (British India) troopship (capacity 1,760 troops) - embarkation at London (King George V Dock), left Thames 6th for Solent (where held in error, having been intended for Convoy EWP1 ETA 8th), left Solent, ETA Gold 12th (Convoy EXP4): returned same night

PAMPAS   8,244/44   Br (Royal Mail) cargo vessel as reserve LSI(L) (capacity 1,525 troops) - arrived Thames 31st May, left 12th for Solent, left Southampton 19th, left Solent (after 2-day delay owing to bad weather), ETA Gold 22nd (Convoy EXP12W): returned to Plymouth

PRINCE BAUDOUIN   3,219/34   Belgian cross-Channel passenger vessel as HM LSI(S) (capacity 384 troops: carried 8 landing craft) - embarkation at anchorage from landing craft from Weymouth, left Weymouth Bay (Anchorage G3) 5th, arrived Omaha 0334 6th (Force J4[O4]) (Assault Convoy O1): 1638 6th left for Solent where arrived 2326 same day

PRINCE CHARLES   2,950/30   Belgian cross-Channel passenger vessel as HM LSI(S) (capacity 270 troops: carried 8 landing craft) - embarkation at anchorage from landing craft from Weymouth, left Weymouth Bay (Anchorage G2) 5th, arrived Omaha 0328 6th (Force J4[O4]) (Assault Convoy O1): left for Solent 1540 6th

PRINCE DAVID   6,892/30   Canadian passenger vessel as Canadian LSI(M) (capacity 468 troops: carried 8 landing craft) - after embarkation, left Southampton (Berth 38) 1650 2nd, left Solent (Anchorage 7/1) 2140 5th, arrived Juno 0617 6th (Force J2) (Assault Convoy J10): returned to Southampton (Berth 40) where arrived 2245 6th

PRINCE HENRY   6,893/30   Canadian passenger vessel NORTH STAR as Canadian LSI(M) (carried 8 landing craft) - after embarkation, left Southampton (Berth 37) 2nd, left Solent (Anchorage 18/7) 2110 5th, arrived Juno 0606 6th (Force J1) (Assault Convoy J9): returned to Solent where arrived 2320 6th

PRINCE LEOPOLD   2,950/30   Belgian cross-Channel passenger vessel as HM LSI(S) (capacity 266 troops: carried 8 landing craft) - embarkation at anchorage from landing craft from Weymouth, left Weymouth Bay (Anchorage G4) 5th, arrived Omaha 0336 6th (Force J4[O4]) (Assault Convoy O1): 1620 6th left for Solent where arrived 2210 same day

PRINCESS MARGARET   2,552/31   Br (London Midland & Scottish Railway) cross-Channel passenger vessel as LSI(H) (capacity 454 troops: carried 6 landing craft) - in April, switched roles with PRINCESS MAUD, embarkation at Solent (Anchorage 7/8), left Spithead Gate 1230 6th, arrived Sword 1830 same day to land commandos attacking the coastal defence battery at Benerville (Force J4)

PRINCE HENRY [IWM A21733]

SAMUEL CHASE [IWM]

PRINCESS MAUD   2,883/34   Br (London Midland & Scottish Railway) cross-Channel passenger vessel as LSI(H) (capacity 487 troops: carried 6 landing craft) - needed repairs after April collision, so switched roles with PRINCESS MARGARET, embarkation at anchorage from landing craft from Weymouth, left Weymouth Bay (Anchorage G6) 5th, arrived Omaha 6th (Force J4[O4]) (Assault Convoy O1)

PRINS ALBERT   2,938/37   Belgian cross-Channel passenger vessel as HM LSI(S) (capacity 507 troops: carried 8 landing craft) - embarkation at Solent (Anchorage 7/7), left Spithead Gate 1230 6th, arrived Sword 1830 same day to land commandos attacking the coastal defence battery at Benerville (Force J4)

PRINSES ASTRID   2,950/30   Belgian cross-Channel passenger vessel as HM LSI(S) (capacity 247 troops: carried 8 landing craft) - after embarkation, left Southampton (Berth 40) 3rd, left Solent (Anchorage 22/a11) 2110 5th, arrived Sword 0542 6th (Force J4) (Assault Convoy S7)

PRINSES JOSEPHINE CHARLOTTE   2,950/31   Belgian cross-Channel passenger vessel as HM LSI(S) (capacity 210 troops: carried 8 landing craft) - embarkation at Southampton (Berth 39), left Solent (Anchorage 7/9) 5th, arrived Gold 6th (Force J4) (Assault Convoy G9E)

QUEEN EMMA   4,135/39   Dutch (Zeeland) cross-Channel passenger vessel KONINGIN EMMA as HM LSI(M) (capacity 372 troops: carried 8 landing craft) - embarkation at Southampton (Berth 40), left Solent (Anchorage 22/c1) 5th, arrived Juno 6th (Force J1) (Assault Convoy J9): returned to Solent

ST HELIER   1,952/25   Br (Great Western Railway) cross-Channel passenger vessel as HM LSI(H) (capacity 420 troops: carried 6 landing craft) - embarkation at Southampton (Berth 40), left Solent (Anchorage 18/2) 5th, arrived Juno 6th (Force J2) (Assault Convoy J10): returned to Plymouth

SAMUEL CHASE   10,812/42   US APA (capacity 1,867 troops: carried 29 landing craft) - embarkation at anchorage from landing craft from Weymouth, left Portland Harbour (Anchorage DD5) 1727 5th, arrived Omaha 0315 6th (Force O1) (Assault Convoy O1): left 2000 6th for Portland where arrived 1500 7th

SEA PORPOISE 10,584/44 US troopship (capacity 2,500 troops) - left Belfast Lough, ETA Utah 3rd July (Convoy EMP1): damaged by mine on leaving at 2108 5th July

SUSAN B. ANTHONY 8,101/30 US (Grace) passenger/cargo liner SANTA CLARA as troopship (capacity 2,288 troops) - embarkation at Newport, left Bristol Channel 5th, ETA Omaha 7th (Convoy EBP1/B3): struck mine 7th while approaching beach-head, shipping water badly and causing a fire; all 2,200 troops and crew had been transferred to LCTs and MENDIP by the time vessel sank at 1010

THOMAS JEFFERSON 9,260/41 US APA (capacity 1,492 troops: carried 34 landing craft) - embarkation at anchorage from landing craft from Weymouth, left Portland Harbour (Anchorage DD2) 5th, arrived Omaha 6th (Force O2) (Assault Convoy O1)

THURSTON 6,509/42 US (Mississippi) vessel as XAP (capacity 1,175 troops: carried 24 landing craft) - embarkation at anchorage from landing craft from Weymouth, left Portland Harbour (Anchorage CC3) 5th, arrived Omaha 6th (Force O3) (Assault Convoy O1)

ULSTER MONARCH 3,791/29 Br (Belfast SS) cross-Channel passenger vessel as HM LSI(H) (capacity 580 troops: carried 6 landing craft) - embarkation at Southampton (Berth 39), left Solent (Anchorage 22/c2) 5th, arrived Juno 6th (Force J1) (Assault Convoy J9): returned to Plymouth

VICTORIA 1,641/07 Br (Isle of Man Steam Packet) cross-Channel passenger vessel as LSI(H) (capacity 320 troops: carried 6 landing craft) - embarkation at Southampton (Berth 37), left Solent (Anchorage 7/10) 5th, arrived Gold 6th (Force J4) (Assault Convoy G9E): returned to Weymouth Bay where arrived 7th

WORCESTERSHIRE 11,402/31 Br (Bibby) passenger/cargo liner as troopship - after embarking about 2,630 troops at London (Tilbury Landing Stage) 2000-2255 4th, left 5th, left Thames 6th, left Solent, arrived Juno 8th (Convoy EWP1): left 2000 8th

ULSTER MONARCH [IWM A21805]

Liberty ships anchored off the beach-head on 7th June, 1944. [IWM B5209]

Section A2 - MECHANISED TRANSPORT (MT) SHIPS, LARGE MILITARY STORE SHIPS AND COMMODITY LOADERS.

The prime function of the MT ships, most of which were of the American-built Liberty type, was to carry approximately 120 army vehicles and 480 men. They sailed from Belfast, from the Bristol Channel ports of Avonmouth, Barry, Cardiff, Newport and Swansea, from Falmouth and Plymouth in the West Country as well as from Southampton, London and the east coast terminals of Hull and Middlesbrough.

NAME OF VESSEL   Tonnage/year of build, nationality (owner), type - origin and/or assembly area, destination and convoy of first sailing: other information. (All dates are June 1944 unless otherwise stated.)

A. FRANK LEVER   7,198/43   US Liberty type - completed loading 0900 and left London 1445 11th, left Thames, ETA Sword 14th (Convoy ETM8): returned to Thames (ETA 18th)

ABIEL FOSTER   7,176/42   US Liberty type - loaded at Newport, left Bristol Channel, via Solent, ETA Utah 8th (Convoy EBM3): returned to Southampton

ALCOA TRADER   4,986/20   US (Alcoa) commodity vessel - left Milford Haven 16th, left Falmouth 1730 18th, ETA Omaha 19th (Convoy ECM11)

AMOS G. THROOP   7,176/42   US Liberty type - loaded at Newport, left Bristol Channel, via Solent, ETA Utah 8th (Convoy EBM3): returned to Southampton

ANGLO INDIAN   5,609/38   Br (Reardon Smith) - after loading, left Hull 20th, anchored Thames 21st, left 26th, arrived Gold 27th (Convoy ETM18)

ARTHUR SEWALL   7,176/44   US Liberty type - after loading, left Plymouth, ETA Omaha 11th (Convoy ECM3): returned to Solent

BELVA LOCKWOOD   7,176/43   US Liberty type - loaded at Southampton, left Solent, ETA Omaha 11th (Convoy ECM3W): returned to Southampton

BENJAMIN HAWKINS   7,191/42   US Liberty type - loaded at Cardiff, left Bristol Channel 1130 5th, arrived Utah 0800 7th (Convoy EBM2): returned to Plymouth where arrived 1628 11th

BERING   7,631/20   US (Alaska Packers) commodity vessel - ex Bristol Channel, left Falmouth 1730 17th, ETA Omaha 18th (Convoy ECM10)

BRADFORD CITY   7,266/43   Br (Reardon Smith) - left Thames 0700 8th, arrived Juno 0805 9th (Convoy ETM3)

CASIMIR PULASKI   7,176/43   US Liberty type - completed loading 1300 and left London 1445 11th, left Thames, ETA Juno 13th (Convoy ETM7)

CHARLES C. JONES   7,198/43   US Liberty type - loaded at Cardiff, left Bristol Channel, via Solent, ETA Utah 8th (Convoy EBM3): returned to Southampton

CHARLES D. POSTON   7,176/43   US Liberty type - loaded at Cardiff, left Bristol Channel, via Solent, ETA Utah 8th (Convoy EBM3): returned to Southampton

CHARLES M. HALL   7,181/42   US Liberty type - loaded at Newport, left Bristol Channel 1130 5th, arrived Omaha 0800 7th (Convoy EBM2)

CHARLES MORGAN   7,244/43   US Liberty type - after loading, left Newport 5th, via Solent, ETA Utah 8th (Convoy EBM3): hit by bomb in No.5 hold 0405 10th, stern settled on bottom in Utah inner anchorage

CHARLES SUMNER   7,176/43   US Liberty type - loaded at Barry, left Bristol Channel 1130 5th, arrived Utah (after being switched from Omaha) 0800 7th (Convoy EBM2)

CHARLES W. ELIOT   7,176/43   US Liberty type - loaded at London, left Thames 0600 7th, ETA Gold 8th (Convoy ETM2): on a subsequent voyage, at 0800 28th, after discharging cargo at Juno, sunk by mine while moving to return assembly anchorage

CHARLES WILLSON PEALE   7,176/42   US Liberty type - after loading, left Barry 2nd, left Bristol Channel 1130 5th, arrived Omaha 0800 7th (Convoy EBM2): returned to Southampton

CHESTER VALLEY   5,078/19   US (Lykes) commodity vessel - ex Bristol Channel, left Falmouth 1830 27th, ETA Omaha 28th (Convoy ECM16)

CLARA BARTON   7,176/42   US Liberty type - loaded at Newport, left Bristol Channel, via Solent, ETA Utah 8th (Convoy EBM3): returned to Solent

CLINTON KELLY   7,176/43   US Liberty type - loaded at Barry, left Bristol Channel, via Solent, ETA Omaha 8th (Convoy EBM3): returned to Southampton

CLYDE L. SEAVEY   7,176/43   US Liberty type - replaced early June by RICHARD HENRY LEE

COLLIS P. HUNTINGTON   7,177/42   US Liberty type - loaded at Cardiff, left Bristol Channel, via Solent, ETA Utah 8th (Convoy EBM3): returned to Southampton

COOMBE HILL   7,268/42   Br (Putney Hill) - left Thames 0630 10th, ETA Juno 11th (Convoy ETM5): on a subsequent voyage, damaged by gunfire at Sword 22nd

COTTON MATHER   7,200/42   US Liberty type - left Thames, ETA Gold 14th (Convoy ETM8)

CYRUS H.K. CURTIS   7,176/43   US Liberty type - loaded at London, left Thames 0600 7th, ETA Juno 8th (Convoy ETM2)

CYRUS H.K. CURTIS in September 1943. [NMM P21854]

CYRUS H. McCORMICK 7,181/42   US Liberty type - loaded at Southampton, left Solent, ETA Western Task Force area 9th (Convoy ECM1W): returned to Southampton

DAN BEARD 7,176/43   US Liberty type - loaded at Southampton, left Solent, ETA Omaha 10th (Convoy ECM2W): returned to Southampton

DAVID CALDWELL 7,176/43   US Liberty type - loaded at Southampton, left Solent, ETA Western Task Force area 12th (Convoy ECM4W): returned, via Solent, to Belfast Lough

DAVID STARR JORDAN 7,176/43   US Liberty type - loaded at Southampton, left Solent, ETA Western Task Force area 9th (Convoy ECM1W)

DEMETERTON 7,344/44   Br (Carlton) - left Thames, ETA Juno 12th (Convoy ETM6): on a subsequent voyage, damaged by gunfire 20th

DERRYCUNIHY 7,093/44   Br (McCowen & Gross) - left Thames, ETA Gold 12th (Convoy ETM6): on a subsequent voyage, at 0735 24th, struck mine in Sword area while en route for Juno with 583 troops and their vehicles: with back broken, after end submerged immediately but remaining part kept afloat by SALVICTOR long enough to discharge vehicles

DUNKELD 4,944/37   Br (Stanhope) - after loading, left London 25th, left Thames 2nd July, ETA Gold 3rd July (Convoy ETM24)

EDWARD D. WHITE 7,176/43   US Liberty type - loaded at Southampton, left Solent, ETA Omaha 11th (Convoy ECM3W): returned to Southampton

EDWARD M. HOUSE 7,240/43   US Liberty type - loaded at Southampton, left Solent, ETA Western Task Force area 12th (Convoy ECM4W): on a subsequent voyage, damaged and flooded forward by U-boat *[U-984]* torpedo 29th but completed voyage to Utah

EDWARD W. SCRIPPS 7,176/43   US Liberty type - loaded at Newport, left Bristol Channel 1130 5th, arrived Omaha 0800 7th (Convoy EBM2)

EDWIN ABBEY 7,176/43   US Liberty type - after loading, left Barry 2nd, left Bristol Channel 1130 5th, arrived Utah 0800 7th (Convoy EBM2): returned to Falmouth where arrived 1945 11th

EDWIN L. DRAKE 7,176/43   US Liberty type - after loading, left Avonmouth 12th, left Falmouth 1730 16th, ETA Omaha 17th (Convoy ECM9)

ELIHU ROOT 7,176/43   US Liberty type - loaded at Southampton, left Solent, ETA Western Task Force area 9th (Convoy ECM1W)

ELMER A. SPERRY 7,176/42   US Liberty type - loaded at Southampton, left Solent, ETA Western Task Force area 12th (Convoy ECM4W)

EMPIRE BRUTUS 7,233/43   Br (MoWT) - left Thames 0630 10th, ETA Juno 11th (Convoy ETM5)

EMPIRE CALL 7,067/44   Br (MoWT) - left Thames, ETA Gold 10th (Convoy ETM4)

EMPIRE CANYON 7,058/43   Br (MoWT) - left Thames, ETA Juno 13th (Convoy ETM7)

EMPIRE CAPULET 7,044/43   Br (MoWT) - left Thames, arrived Sword 13th (Convoy ETM7): barge alongside vessel hit by bomb 13th

EMPIRE CELIA 7,025/43   Br (MoWT) - left Thames 0630 10th, ETA Gold 11th (Convoy ETM5)

EMPIRE DARING 7,059/43   Br (MoWT) - arrived London 13th to load, left 24th, left Thames 30th, ETA Eastern Task Force area 1st July (Convoy ETM22)

EMPIRE DEED 6,766/43   Br (MoWT) - loaded at London (Berth J, Millwall Dock), left Thames, ETA Juno 10th (Convoy ETM4)

EMPIRE DUKE 7,240/43   Br (MoWT) - completed loading 2200 10th and left London 1545 11th, left Thames, ETA Juno 13th (Convoy ETM7)

EMPIRE EARL 7,359/44   Br (MoWT) - left Thames 0700 8th, arrived Gold 0805 9th (Convoy ETM3)

EMPIRE FALSTAFF   7,067/43   Br (MoWT) - left Thames, ETA Juno 12th (Convoy ETM6)

EMPIRE FARMER   7,049/43   Br (MoWT) - left Thames, ETA Sword 13th (Convoy ETM7)

EMPIRE GENERAL   7,359/44   Br (MoWT) - left Thames 0700 8th, arrived Juno 0805 9th (Convoy ETM3)

EMPIRE GLADSTONE   7,090/44   Br (MoWT) - left Thames, ETA Gold 12th (Convoy ETM6)

EMPIRE GREY   6,140/44   Br (MoWT) - left Thames, ETA Gold 12th (Convoy ETM6)

EMPIRE HEYWOOD   7,030/42   Br (MoWT) - left Thames, ETA Juno 13th (Convoy ETM7)

EMPIRE LANKESTER   7,067/44   Br (MoWT) - left Thames, ETA Juno 12th (Convoy ETM6)

EMPIRE MANDARIN   7,078/44   Br (MoWT) - arrived Middlesbrough 11th to load, left 22nd, left Thames 30th, ETA Gold 1st July (Convoy ETM22)

EMPIRE NEWTON   7,037/42   Br (MoWT) - left Thames 0630 10th, ETA Juno 11th (Convoy ETM5)

EMPIRE PERDITA   7,028/43   Br (MoWT) - after loading, left Hull 21st, left Thames 27th, arrived Gold 28th (Convoy ETM19)

EMPIRE PICKWICK   7,068/43   Br (MoWT) - left Thames, ETA Juno 10th (Convoy ETM4)

EMPIRE PITT   7,086/44   Br (MoWT) - left Thames, ETA Gold 12th (Convoy ETM6): in collision with BULOLO 15th

EMPIRE PLOUGHMAN   7,049/43   Br (MoWT) - loaded at London (Berth F, Royal Victoria Dock), left Thames, ETA Gold 10th (Convoy ETM4)

EMPIRE PORTIA   7,058/42   Br (MoWT) - left Thames 0700 8th, arrived Juno 0805 9th (Convoy ETM3): on a subsequent voyage, engine room flooded by mine explosion 29th, vessel towed to Solent

EMPIRE RHODES   7,030/41   Br (MoWT) - left Thames 0630 10th, ETA Juno 11th (Convoy ETM5)

EMPIRE PERDITA [IWM MH2407]

EMPIRE STUART   7,067/44   Br (MoWT) - loaded at London (Berth 13, Royal Albert Dock), left Thames, ETA Gold 10th (Convoy ETM4)

ENOCH TRAIN   7,176/43   US Liberty type - loaded at Newport, left Bristol Channel, via Solent, ETA Utah 8th (Convoy EBM3): returned to Southampton

EPHRAIM BREVARD   7,177/43   US Liberty type - loaded at Newport, left Bristol Channel 1130 5th, arrived Omaha 0800 7th (Convoy EBM2): returned to Southampton

EUGENE E. O'DONNELL   7,176/43   US Liberty type - loaded at Cardiff, left Bristol Channel, via Solent, ETA Utah 8th (Convoy EBM3): returned to Southampton

EZRA WESTON   7,176/43   US Liberty type - loaded at Cardiff, left Bristol Channel 1130 5th, arrived Utah 0800 7th (Convoy EBM2): returned to Southampton

FLORENCE CRITTENTON   7,176/43   US Liberty type - loaded at Southampton, left Solent, ETA Utah 10th (Convoy ECM2W)

FORT ASSINIBOINE   7,128/43   Br (MoWT) Canadian - left Thames 0630 10th, ETA Gold 11th (Convoy ETM5)

FORT AUGUSTUS   7,134/42   Br (MoWT) US - after loading, left Hull, left Thames 14th, arrived Eastern Task Force area 15th (Convoy ETM9)

FORT BEDFORD   7,127/43   Br (MoWT) US - left Thames, ETA Gold 13th (Convoy ETM7)

FORT BILOXI   7,161/43   Br (MoWT) Canadian - loaded at London, left Thames 0600 7th, ETA Juno 8th (Convoy ETM2): returned to London where arrived 1820 11th

FORT BRUNSWICK   7,141/44   Br (MoWT) Canadian - left Thames, ETA Juno 10th (Convoy ETM4)

FORT CHARNISAY   7,133/43   Br (MoWT) US - left Thames 0700 8th, arrived Sword 0805 9th (Convoy ETM3)

FORT CHIPEWYAN   7,136/42   Br (MoWT) US - after loading, left Hull 12th, anchored Thames 13th, left 14th, arrived Eastern Task Force area 15th (Convoy ETM9)

FORT CREVECOEUR   7,191/43   Br (MoWT) Canadian - loaded at London, left Thames 0600 7th, ETA Gold 8th (Convoy ETM2)

FORT DEARBORN   7,160/44   Br (MoWT) Canadian - loaded at London, left Thames 0600 7th, ETA Gold 8th (Convoy ETM2)

FORT ESPERANCE   7,138/43   Br (MoWT) Canadian - loaded at London (Berth B, Royal Victoria Dock), left Thames, ETA Gold 10th (Convoy ETM4)

FORT FINLAY   7,134/43   Br (MoWT) US - left Thames, ETA Juno 12th (Convoy ETM6)

FORT FORK   7,134/42   Br (MoWT) US - completed loading 1030 and left London 1530 11th, left Thames, ETA Sword 13th (Convoy ETM7)

FORT GIBRALTAR   7,134/42   Br (MoWT) US - left Thames, ETA Juno 10th (Convoy ETM4)

FORT HENLEY   7,138/43   Br (MoWT) Canadian - left Thames 0700 8th, arrived Gold 0805 9th (Convoy ETM3)

FORT KASKASKIA   7,187/43   Br (MoWT) Canadian - loaded at London, left Thames 0600 7th, ETA Gold 8th (Convoy ETM2)

FORT LAC LA RONGE   7,131/42   Br (MoWT) US - after loading, left Hull 15th, left Thames 17th, arrived Sword 18th (Convoy ETM12)

FORT LIVINGSTONE   7,135/42   Br (MoWT) US - left Thames 0630 10th, ETA Gold 11th (Convoy ETM5)

FORT McMURRAY   7,133/42   Br (MoWT) US - left Thames 0630 10th, ETA Juno 11th (Convoy ETM5): damaged by grounding at Sword 18th, returned to London (Berth 32, Tilbury Dock) for repairs

FORT YUKON [NMM P22756]

FORT McPHERSON 7,132/43 Br (MoWT) Canadian - left Thames 0630 10th, ETA Juno 11th (Convoy ETM5) to discharge approx 670 troops and their vehicles: 0330 11th damaged by a glider bomb, left 2000 12th for Southampton where arrived 13th thence to London 17th

FORT NORFOLK 7,131/43 Br (MoWT) Canadian - left Thames 0700 8th, arrived Juno 0805 9th (Convoy ETM3): on a subsequent voyage, at 0817 24th, after discharging cargo at Juno, struck mine while moving to return assembly anchorage: engine room and stokehold completely wrecked and flooded, within an hour stern broke off and sank, leaving bows protruding above the water

FORT ORANGE 7,176/43 Dutch US Liberty type commodity vessel - ex Bristol Channel, left Falmouth 1830 25th, ETA Omaha 26th (Convoy ECM14)

FORT PIC 7,150/43 Br (MoWT) Canadian - left Thames 0700 8th, arrived Gold 0830 9th (Convoy ETM3): 2245 9th, superficially damaged above waterline by small bomb, commenced discharge of troops and vehicles 13th then sailed for Solent thence to London for repairs

FORT POPLAR 7,134/42 Br (MoWT) US - left Thames 0630 10th, ETA Juno 11th (Convoy ETM5): grounded 1915 19th but later pulled off, returned to London (Berth 9/10, Tilbury Dock) for repairs 28th

FORT RAE 7,132/42 Br (MoWT) US - after loading, left London 18th, left Thames, ETA Gold 20th (Convoy ETM14)

FORT RELIANCE 7,134/42 Br (MoWT) US - left Thames 0630 10th, ETA Gold 11th (Convoy ETM5)

FORT ROMAINE 7,131/43 Br (MoWT) Canadian - left Thames, ETA Sword 12th (Convoy ETM6)

FORT ST. CROIX 7,160/43 Br (MoWT) Canadian - loaded at London, left Thames 0600 7th, ETA Juno 8th (Convoy ETM2): returned to London where arrived 1855 11th

FORT SLAVE 7,134/42 Br (MoWT) US - left Thames 0700 8th, arrived Juno 0805 9th (Convoy ETM3)

FORT TICONDEROGA 7,138/43 Br (MoWT) Canadian - after loading, left Hull 29th, left Thames 6th July, arrived Eastern Task Force area 7th July (Convoy ETM28)

FORT TREMBLANT 7,128/42 Br (MoWT) US - left Thames 0630 10th, ETA Juno 11th (Convoy ETM5)

FORT WALLACE 7,161/44 Br (MoWT) Canadian - loaded at London, left Thames 0600 7th, ETA Juno 8th (Convoy ETM2)

FORT WRIGLEY 7,128/43 Br (MoWT) Canadian - left Thames 0630 10th, ETA Gold 11th (Convoy ETM5)

FORT YALE 7,134/42 Br (MoWT) US - left Thames 0630 10th, ETA Gold 11th (Convoy ETM5)

FORT YUKON 7,153/43 Br (MoWT) Canadian - after loading, left Hull 27th, left Thames 4th July, arrived Eastern Task Force area 5th July (Convoy ETM26)

FRANCIS ASBURY 7,176/43   US Liberty type - after loading, left Falmouth, ETA Utah 11th (Convoy ECM3): returned to Falmouth

FRANCIS C. HARRINGTON 7,176/43   US Liberty type - loaded at Newport, left Bristol Channel 1130 5th, arrived Omaha 0800 7th (Convoy EBM2): damaged by mine 7th: completed discharge 11th: returned to Middlesbrough where arrived 19th

FRANCIS DRAKE 7,176/42   US Liberty type - after loading, left Falmouth, ETA Utah 12th (Convoy ECM4): returned to Falmouth

FRANK B. KELLOGG 7,176/42   US Liberty type - ex Milford Haven, left Portland, ETA Utah 1st July (Convoy ECM19P)

FRANK R. STOCKTON 7,176/43   US Liberty type - loaded at Newport, left Bristol Channel 1130 5th, arrived Utah 0800 7th (Convoy EBM2)

G. W. GOETHALS 7,176/42   US Liberty type - loaded at Southampton, left Solent, ETA Utah 10th (Convoy ECM2W)

GEORGE DEWEY 7,225/43   US Liberty type - loaded at Southampton, left Solent, ETA Western Task Force area 12th (Convoy ECM4W): returned to Southampton

GEORGE DURANT 7,176/43   US Liberty type - left Thames 0700 8th, arrived Juno 0805 9th (Convoy ETM3)

GEORGE E. BADGER 7,177/43   US Liberty type - loaded at Southampton, left Solent, ETA Western Task Force area 9th (Convoy ECM1W)

GEORGE E. PICKETT 7,244/43   US Liberty type - loaded at Newport, left Bristol Channel 1130 5th, arrived Utah 0800 7th (Convoy EBM2)

GEORGE G. CRAWFORD 7,198/44   US Liberty type - loaded at Southampton, left Solent, ETA Western Task Force area 9th (Convoy ECM1W)

GEORGE STEERS 7,247/44   US Liberty type - loaded at Southampton, left Solent, ETA Omaha 11th (Convoy ECM3W): returned to Southampton

GEORGE WHITEFIELD 7,176/43   US Liberty type - loaded at Southampton, left Solent, ETA Western Task Force area 9th (Convoy ECM1W): returned, via Solent, to Belfast Lough

GEORGE WYTHE 7,191/42   US Liberty type - loaded at London, left Thames 0600 7th, ETA Gold 8th (Convoy ETM2)

GREENWICH 7,292/43   Br (Britain SS) - after loading, left Hull 28th, left Thames 4th July, arrived Eastern Task Force area 5th July (Convoy ETM26)

H. G. BLASDEL 7,176/43   US Liberty type - loaded at Southampton, left Solent, ETA Utah 10th (Convoy ECM2W): returned to Southampton: on a subsequent voyage to Utah, torpedoed by U-boat *[U-984]* 29th and, with engine room and No.5 hold flooded, towed to Solent by tug AMSTERDAM for discharge of cargo. *[Not repaired]*

HANNIBAL HAMLIN 7,176/43   US Liberty type - loaded at London, left Thames 0600 7th, ETA Juno 8th (Convoy ETM2)

HARRY PERCY 7,244/43   US Liberty type - loaded at Southampton, left Solent, ETA Western Task Force area 9th (Convoy ECM1W): returned to Southampton

HELLAS 7,176/43   Greek US Liberty type - loaded at Barry, left Bristol Channel, via Solent, ETA Omaha 8th (Convoy EBM3): returned to Southampton

HENRY AUSTIN 7,244/43   US Liberty type - loaded at London, left Thames 0600 7th, ETA Juno 8th (Convoy ETM2)

HENRY M. RICE 7,176/43   US Liberty type - after loading, left Plymouth 9th, ETA Omaha 10th (Convoy ECM2): returned to Plymouth

Army gun-towing vehicles ready for loading aboard a Liberty ship.
[IWM B5214]

HENRY S. LANE 7,176/43 US Liberty type - loaded at Southampton, left Solent, ETA Utah 10th (Convoy ECM2W)

HENRY W. GRADY 7,201/43 US Liberty type - loaded at Barry, left Bristol Channel 1130 5th, arrived Omaha 0800 7th (Convoy EBM2): returned to Southampton

HENRY WYNKOOP 7,176/42 US Liberty type - arrived Avonmouth 9th to load, left Falmouth, ETA Omaha 3rd July (Convoy EMM1)

HERMAN MELVILLE 7,176/42 US Liberty type - arrived Avonmouth 8th to load, left Falmouth, ETA Western Task Force area 3rd July (Convoy EMM1) for onward routing to Cherbourg

HORACE GRAY 7,200/43 US Liberty type - loaded at Newport, left Bristol Channel 1130 5th, arrived Omaha 0800 7th (Convoy EBM2)

HORACE WILLIAMS 7,176/43 US Liberty type - replaced early June by OLIVER EVANS

HOUSTON CITY 7,262/42 Br (Reardon Smith) - (movements unclear) arrived London 20th (Convoy FTM12 possibly ex beach-head): left London 23rd, left Thames 26th (possibly for beach-head)

HUTCHINSON I. CONE 7,176/43 US Liberty type - after loading, left Avonmouth 13th, left Falmouth 1730 16th, ETA Utah 17th (Convoy ECM9)

IGNATIUS DONNELLY 7,176/43 US Liberty type - loaded at London, left Thames 0600 7th, ETA Gold 8th (Convoy ETM2)

IMPERIAL VALLEY 4,573/24 Br (Reardon Smith) - after loading, left Middlesbrough 18th, left Thames 27th, arrived Sword 28th (Convoy ETM19)

INDIAN CITY 7,079/44 Br (Reardon Smith) - left Thames, ETA Juno 13th (Convoy ETM7)

J. D. ROSS 7,176/43 US Liberty type - loaded at Southampton, left Solent, ETA Western Task Force area 9th (Convoy ECM1W)

J. E. B. STUART 7,196/42 US Liberty type - after loading, left Falmouth 0205 12th, ETA Utah 13th (Convoy ECM5)

J. WARREN KEIFER 7,176/43   US Liberty type commodity vessel - left Oban 24th, left Falmouth 1830 27th, ETA Utah 28th (Convoy ECM16)

JAMES A. FARRELL 7,176/43   US Liberty type - loaded at Southampton, left Solent, ETA Utah 10th (Convoy ECM2W): returned to Southampton: on a subsequent voyage to Utah, hit aft abreast mainmast by U-boat *[U-984]* torpedo 29th, crew taken off by LST 50: vessel found abandoned and drifting by frigate DACRES: down by the stern, with hold Nos.3 and 5 flooded, towed to Solent firstly by CALDY then by ZWARTE ZEE for beaching on 3rd July and discharge of cargo. *[Not repaired]*

JAMES B. WEAVER 7,176/43   US Liberty type - after loading, left Falmouth, ETA Utah 10th (Convoy ECM2): shot down a glider bomb 10th: returned to Falmouth where arrived 1315 13th

JAMES CALDWELL 7,191/42   US Liberty type - loaded at Southampton, left Solent, ETA Utah 10th (Convoy ECM2W): returned to Southampton

JAMES I. McKAY 7,176/43   US Liberty type - after loading, left Falmouth, ETA Utah 12th (Convoy ECM4): returned to Falmouth

JAMES L. ACKERSON 7,240/44   US Liberty type - loaded at Southampton, left Solent, ETA Western Task Force area 9th (Convoy ECM1W)

JAMES R. RANDALL 7,176/43   US Liberty type - arrived Belfast Lough 14th to load, left 1530 23rd, left Falmouth 1830 26th, ETA Omaha 27th (Convoy ECM15)

JAMES WOODROW 7,200/42   US Liberty type - loaded at Southampton, left Solent, ETA Western Task Force area 12th (Convoy ECM4W): returned to Southampton

JANE G. SWISSHELM 7,176/43   US Liberty type - after loading, left Newport 1st July, arrived Falmouth 3rd July, left, ETA Omaha 4th July (Convoy ECM21)

JANE LONG 7,244/43   US Liberty type - loaded at Southampton, left Solent, ETA Western Task Force area 12th (Convoy ECM4W): returned to Southampton

JEDEDIAH S. SMITH 7,176/43   US Liberty type - loaded at Newport, left Bristol Channel 1130 5th, arrived Utah 0800 7th (Convoy EBM2)

JEREMIAH O'BRIEN 7,176/43   US Liberty type - loaded at Southampton, left Solent, ETA Omaha 10th (Convoy ECM2W): returned to Southampton. *[Vessel now preserved at San Francisco]*

JESSE APPLEGATE 7,176/42   US Liberty type - ex Plymouth for Western Task Force area (intended for Convoy ECM1 ETA 9th): returned to Plymouth 14th

JIM BRIDGER 7,180/42   US Liberty type - after loading, left Plymouth, ETA Omaha 12th (Convoy ECM4)

JOHN A. CAMPBELL 7,176/43   US Liberty type - loaded at Southampton, left Solent, ETA Utah 10th (Convoy ECM2W): returned to Southampton

JOHN A. SUTTER 7,176/42   US Liberty type - loaded at London, left Thames 0600 7th, ETA Sword 8th (Convoy ETM2)

JOHN A. TREUTLEN 7,198/44   US Liberty type - loaded at Cardiff, left Falmouth 1800 28th, ETA Omaha 29th (Convoy ECM17), en route damaged by U-boat *[U-984]* torpedo and, slightly down by the stern, with hold Nos.3 and 5 flooded and No.1 leaking, towed to Solent by tug FARALLON for beaching and discharge of cargo. *[Not repaired]*

JOHN E. SWEET 7,198/44   US Liberty type - loaded at London, left Thames 0600 7th, ETA Juno 8th (Convoy ETM2)

JOHN E. WARD 7,198/43   US Liberty type - loaded at London, left Thames 0600 7th, ETA Gold 8th (Convoy ETM2)

JOHN F. STEFFEN 7,176/43   US Liberty type - loaded at Southampton, left Solent, ETA Utah 12th (Convoy ECM4W)

The Liberty ship on the left has sunk by the stern. [IWM]

JOHN G. WHITTIER 7,176/42 US Liberty type - loaded at Southampton, left Solent, ETA Western Task Force area 12th (Convoy ECM4W): returned to Southampton

JOHN HAY 7,176/43 US Liberty type - loaded at Barry, left Bristol Channel, via Solent, ETA Omaha 8th (Convoy EBM3): completed discharge 11th and returned to Plymouth where arrived 0740 13th

JOHN HENRY 7,191/42 US Liberty type - after loading, left Plymouth 0529 12th, ETA Utah 13th (Convoy ECM5)

JOHN MERRICK 7,176/43 US Liberty type - loaded at Southampton, left Solent, ETA Omaha 11th (Convoy ECM3W)

JOHN R. PARK 7,184/43 US Liberty type - loaded at Southampton, left Solent, ETA Omaha 11th (Convoy ECM3W): returned to Southampton

JOHN S. MOSBY 7,225/43 US Liberty type - loaded at Cardiff, left Bristol Channel 1130 5th, arrived Utah 0800 7th (Convoy EBM2): returned to Falmouth where arrived 1938 11th

JOHN STEELE 7,176/42 US Liberty type - after loading, left Barry 2nd, left Bristol Channel 1130 5th, arrived Omaha 0800 7th (Convoy EBM2): returned to Southampton

JOSEPH A. BROWN 7,176/43 US Liberty type - arrived Belfast Lough 20th to load, left, ETA Utah 3rd July (Convoy EMM1)

JOSEPH E. JOHNSTON 7,196/42 US Liberty type - loaded at Southampton, left Solent, arrived Omaha 11th (Convoy ECM3W): returned to Southampton

JOSEPH PULITZER 7,176/42 US Liberty type - loaded at Southampton, left Solent, ETA Omaha 11th (Convoy ECM3W): returned to Southampton

JOSEPH STORY 7,176/42 US Liberty type - loaded at Southampton, left Solent, ETA Western Task Force area 12th (Convoy ECM4W)

JOSHUA B. LIPPINCOTT 7,176/43 US Liberty type - loaded at Newport, left Bristol Channel, via Solent, ETA Utah 8th (Convoy EBM3): returned to Southampton

JOSIAH NELSON CUSHING 7,176/43 US Liberty type - loaded at Newport, left Bristol Channel 1130 5th, arrived Utah 0800 7th (Convoy EBM2)

JUAN FLACO BROWN 7,176/43 US Liberty type - after loading, left Avonmouth 12th, left Falmouth 1730 16th, ETA Omaha 17th (Convoy ECM9)

JULIUS ROSENWALD 7,176/43 US Liberty type - arrived Belfast Lough 20th to load, left, ETA Utah 3rd July (Convoy EMM1)

KING EDGAR 4,536/27 Br (King) - loaded at Hull, left Thames 27th, arrived Juno 28th (Convoy ETM19)

LAMBROOK 7,038/42 Br (Austin Friars) - left Thames, ETA Gold 12th (Convoy ETM6)

LANGLEECRAG 4,909/29 Br (Medomsley) - loaded at Hull, left Humber 21st, left Thames 27th, arrived Juno 28th (Convoy ETM19)

LEE S. OVERMAN 7,176/43 US Liberty type - loaded at London, left Thames 0600 7th, ETA Juno 8th (Convoy ETM2)

LEWIS MORRIS   7,181/42   US Liberty type - ex Bristol Channel, left Falmouth 1800 28th, ETA Utah 29th (Convoy ECM17)

LLOYDCREST   7,020/44   Br (Crest) - left Thames, ETA Gold 10th (Convoy ETM4): collided with DIADEM 19th

LOU GEHRIG   7,176/43   US Liberty type - after loading, left Falmouth 0205 12th, ETA Utah 13th (Convoy ECM5)

LOUIS KOSSUTH   7,176/43   US Liberty type - after loading, left Barry 3rd, left Bristol Channel 6th, via Solent, ETA Omaha 8th (Convoy EBM3): returned to Falmouth where arrived 1315 13th

LOUIS MARSHALL   7,176/43   US Liberty type - loaded at Southampton, left Solent, ETA Omaha 10th (Convoy ECM2W): returned to Southampton

LUCIEN B. MAXWELL   7,244/43   US Liberty type - after loading, left Falmouth, ETA Utah 9th (Convoy ECM1): returned to Falmouth

LUCIUS Q.C. LAMAR   7,191/43   US Liberty type - arrived Belfast Lough 20th to load, left, ETA Utah 3rd July (Convoy EMM1)

LUCY STONE   7,176/43   US Liberty type - after loading, left Falmouth, ETA Utah 9th (Convoy ECM1): returned to Falmouth where arrived 1928 11th

LYMAN HALL   7,176/43   US Liberty type - after loading, left Avonmouth 26th, left Falmouth 1800 28th, ETA Omaha 29th (Convoy ECM17)

MALAYAN PRINCE   8,593/26   Br (Rio Cape) - loaded at London (Berth E, Royal Victoria Dock), left Thames, ETA Sword 10th (Convoy ETM4)

MARWARRI   8,067/35   Br (Brocklebank) - left Thames, ETA Juno 10th (Convoy ETM4)

MATTHEW T. GOLDSBORO   7,177/43   US Liberty type - loaded at London, left Thames 0600 7th, ETA Juno 8th (Convoy ETM2)

MELVILLE JACOBY   7,176/44   US Liberty type - loaded at Swansea, left Bristol Channel 17th, left Falmouth, ETA Omaha 20th (Convoy ECM12)

MEXICAN   8,030/07   US commodity vessel - ex Bristol Channel, left Falmouth 1730 17th, ETA Utah 18th (Convoy ECM10)

MONKLEIGH   5,203/27   Br (Atlantic) - after loading, left Hull 18th, left Thames, arrived Juno 25th (Convoy ETM16)

NORTH KING   5,024/03   Panamanian - left Bristol Channel 27th, left Falmouth 1800 28th, ETA Utah 29th (Convoy ECM17)

OCEAN ANGEL   7,178/42   Br (MoWT) - left Thames, ETA Juno 12th (Convoy ETM6)

OCEAN COURIER   7,178/42   Br (MoWT) - loaded at London (Berth M, SW India Dock), left Thames, ETA Gold 10th (Convoy ETM4)

OCEAN STRENGTH   7,173/42   Br (MoWT) - left Thames, ETA Gold 12th (Convoy ETM6)

OCEAN VAGRANT   7,174/42   Br (MoWT) - completed loading 1510 and left London 1650 11th, left Thames, ETA Gold 13th (Convoy ETM7)

OCEAN VENGEANCE   7,174/42   Br (MoWT) - left Thames 0700 8th, arrived Gold 0805 9th (Convoy ETM3)

OCEAN VIGIL   7,174/41   Br (MoWT) - completed loading 1530 and left London 1750 11th, left Thames, ETA Gold 14th (Convoy ETM8)

OCEAN VIGOUR   7,174/42   Br (MoWT) - left Thames, ETA Juno 13th (Convoy ETM7)

OCEAN VISION   7,174/42   Br (MoWT) - left Thames 0700 8th, arrived Gold 0805 9th (Convoy ETM3)

OCEAN VISTA   7,174/42   Br (MoWT) - left Thames, ETA Juno 10th (Convoy ETM4)

OCEAN VOLGA [NMM P23666]

OCEAN VOLGA 7,174/42 Br (MoWT) - left Thames 0700 8th, arrived Gold 0805 9th (Convoy ETM3)

OLIVER EVANS 7,176/43 US Liberty type - after loading, left Cardiff 27th, left Falmouth 29th for Western Task Force area

OLIVER WOLCOTT 7,181/42 US Liberty type - loaded at Cardiff, left Bristol Channel 1130 5th, arrived Omaha 0800 7th (Convoy EBM2)

OMAR E. CHAPMAN 7,176/43 US Liberty type - arrived Belfast Lough 20th to load, left, ETA Utah 3rd July (Convoy EMM1)

ORMINSTER 5,712/14 Br (South American Saint) - after loading, left Hull 18th, arrived Thames 19th, left 24th, arrived Juno 25th (Convoy ETM16)

PANAMAN 5,328/13 US commodity vessel - after loading, left Falmouth 1730 18th, ETA Utah 19th (Convoy ECM11)

PARK BENJAMIN 7,176/44 US Liberty type - loaded at London, left Thames 0600 7th, ETA Juno 8th (Convoy ETM2)

PEARL HARBOR 7,200/42 US Liberty type - loaded at Southampton, left Solent, ETA Western Task Force area 9th (Convoy ECM1W)

PEREGRINE WHITE 7,176/43 US Liberty type commodity vessel - ex Bristol Channel, left Falmouth 1730 17th, ETA Omaha 18th (Convoy ECM10)

REMBRANDT 8,126/41 Dutch - after loading, left Hull 12th, anchored Thames 13th, left 14th, arrived Eastern Task Force area 15th (Convoy ETM9)

RICHARD HENRY LEE 7,191/41 US Liberty type - after loading, left Cardiff 27th, left Falmouth 29th for Western Task Force area

RICHMOND HILL 7,579/40 Br (Putney Hill) - after loading, left Hull 12th, anchored Thames 13th, left 14th, arrived Eastern Task Force area 15th (Convoy ETM9)

ROBERT E. PEARY 7,181/42 US Liberty type - after loading, left Cardiff 2nd, left Bristol Channel 1130 5th, arrived Utah 0800 7th (Convoy EBM2): returned to Falmouth where arrived 11th

ROBERT HENRI 7,244/44 US Liberty type - loaded at London, left Thames 0600 7th, ETA Gold 8th (Convoy ETM2)

ROBERT L. VANN   7,176/43   US Liberty type - loaded at Newport, left Bristol Channel 1130 5th, arrived Omaha 0800 7th (Convoy EBM2)

ROBERT LANSING   7,176/43   US Liberty type - loaded at London, left Thames 0600 7th, ETA Gold 8th (Convoy ETM2)

ROBERT LOWRY   7,176/43   US Liberty type - after loading, left Swansea 15th, left Falmouth, ETA Utah 20th (Convoy ECM12)

ROBERT TOOMBS   7,176/43   US Liberty type - loaded at Southampton, left Solent, ETA Omaha 11th (Convoy ECM3W): returned to Southampton

ROMNEY   5,840/29   Br (Bolton) - after loading, left Hull 17th, left Thames 17th, arrived Gold 18th (Convoy ETM12)

ROYAL S. COPELAND   7,240/44   US Liberty type commodity vessel - left Falmouth 23rd, via Solent, ETA Utah 26th (Convoy ECM14W)

SAM HOUSTON II   7,244/43   US Liberty type - left Thames, ETA Juno 13th (Convoy ETM7)

SAMARK   7,219/43   Br (MoWT) US Liberty type - loaded at London, left Thames 0630 6th, arrived Juno 0700 7th (Convoy ETM1): returned to Thames 9th/10th

SAMAROVSK   7,219/43   Br (MoWT) US Liberty type - loaded at London, left Thames 0630 6th, arrived Juno 0700 7th (Convoy ETM1): returned to Thames 9th/10th

SAMBUT   7,219/43   Br (MoWT) US Liberty type - loaded at London, left Thames 0630 6th, ETA Juno 7th, to discharge approx 560 troops and their vehicles (Convoy ETM1): at 1203 6th hit forward by two shells from shore batteries while transitting the Strait of Dover: vessel set on fire, abandoned at 1240 and sank 1900 same day, east of the Goodwin Sands

SAMDEL   7,219/43   Br (MoWT) US Liberty type - loaded at London, left Thames 0630 6th, arrived Juno 0700 7th (Convoy ETM1)

SAMHOLT   7,219/43   Br (MoWT) US Liberty type - arrived London 16th to load, left 27th, left Thames 2nd July, arrived Juno 3rd July (Convoy ETM24)

SAMINVER   7,210/44   Br (MoWT) US Liberty type - loaded at London, left Thames 0630 6th, arrived Juno 0700 7th (Convoy ETM1): returned to London where arrived 1800 11th

SAMINVER in May 1944. [IWM A23033]

SAMMONT   7,219/43   Br (MoWT) US Liberty type - loaded at London, left Thames 0630 6th, arrived Juno 7th (Convoy ETM1)

SAMNESSE   7,219/43   Br (MoWT) US Liberty type - left Thames 0700 8th, arrived Juno 0805 9th (Convoy ETM3)

SAMNEVA   7,219/43   Br (MoWT) US Liberty type - loaded at London, left Thames 0630 6th, arrived Juno 0700 7th (Convoy ETM1)

SAMOS   7,219/43   Br (MoWT) US Liberty type - loaded at London, left Thames 0630 6th, arrived Juno 0700 7th (Convoy ETM1): returned to Thames where arrived 13th

SAMPEP   7,219/43   Br (MoWT) US Liberty type - loaded at London, left Thames 0630 6th, arrived Juno 0700 7th (Convoy ETM1): returned to Thames 9th/10th

SAMPHILL   7,219/43   Br (MoWT) US Liberty type - loaded at London, left Thames 0630 6th, arrived Juno 0700 7th (Convoy ETM1): returned to Thames 9th/10th

SAMSIP   7,219/43   Br (MoWT) US Liberty type - left Thames, ETA Juno 13th (Convoy ETM7)

SAMUEL COLT   7,176/42   US Liberty type - loaded at Southampton, left Solent, ETA Western Task Force area 12th (Convoy ECM4W): returned to Southampton

SAMUEL McINTYRE   7,176/43   US Liberty type - loaded at Avonmouth, left Bristol Channel, via Falmouth, ETA Utah 1st July (Convoy ECM19) for onward routing to Cherbourg

SAMVERN   7,219/43   Br (MoWT) US Liberty type - loaded at London, left Thames 0630 6th, arrived Juno 0700 7th (Convoy ETM1)

SAMYORK   7,219/43   Br (MoWT) US Liberty type - left Thames, ETA Juno 13th (Convoy ETM7)

SAMZONA   7,219/43   Br (MoWT) US Liberty type - loaded at London, left Thames 0630 6th, arrived Juno 0700 7th (Convoy ETM1): returned to Thames 9th/10th

SIMON NEWCOMB   7,176/43   US Liberty type commodity vessel - ex Bristol Channel, left Falmouth 27th for Omaha

STANRIDGE   5,975/43   Br (Stanhope) - left Thames, ETA Gold 12th (Convoy ETM6)

STANTON H. KING   7,176/44   US Liberty type - arrived Falmouth 6th to load, left, ETA Utah 11th (Convoy ECM3): returned to Falmouth

STEPHEN B. ELKINS   7,180/43   US Liberty type - loaded at Newport, left Bristol Channel 1130 5th, arrived Omaha 0800 7th (Convoy EBM2)

THOMAS HARTLEY   7,176/42   US Liberty type commodity vessel - ex Bristol Channel, left Falmouth 1830 27th, ETA Omaha 28th (Convoy ECM16)

THOMAS J. JARVIS   7,176/43   US Liberty type - arrived Belfast 25th to load, left 28th, ETA Utah 3rd July (Convoy EMM1)

THOMAS KEARNS   7,194/43   US Liberty type - ex Bristol Channel, left Falmouth 29th, arrived Utah 1st July

THOMAS SCOTT   7,176/42   US Liberty type - loaded at Southampton, left Solent, ETA Western Task Force area 9th (Convoy ECM1W)

THOMAS WOLFE   7,198/43   US Liberty type - loaded at Southampton, left Solent, ETA Utah 10th (Convoy ECM2W): returned to Southampton

TREVIDER   7,376/44   Br (Hain) - loaded at London (Berth K, SW India Dock), left Thames, ETA Gold 10th (Convoy ETM4)

VANCOUVER CITY   7,261/42   Br (Reardon Smith) - left Thames, ETA Juno 12th (Convoy ETM6)

WALTER HINES PAGE   7,176/43   US Liberty type - loaded at Newport, left Bristol Channel 1130 5th, arrived Omaha 0800 7th (Convoy EBM2)

WEBB MILLER 7,176/43 US Liberty type - loaded at Cardiff, left Bristol Channel, via Solent, ETA Utah 8th (Convoy EBM3): returned to Southampton

WELSH TRADER 4,974/38 Br (Trader Navigation) - after loading, left London 27th, left Thames 1st July, arrived Juno 2nd July (Convoy ETC24)

WILL ROGERS 7,200/42 US Liberty type - loaded at London, left Thames 0600 7th, ETA Gold 8th (Convoy ETM2)

WILLARD HALL 7,200/43 US Liberty type - loaded at Cardiff, left Falmouth, ETA Utah 4th July (Convoy ECM21)

WILLIAM A. JONES 7,176/43 US Liberty type - loaded at London, left Thames 0600 7th, ETA Sword 8th (Convoy ETM2)

WILLIAM CARSON 7,176/43 US Liberty type - loaded at London, left Thames 0600 7th, ETA Gold 8th (Convoy ETM2)

WILLIAM L. MARCY 7,176/42 US Liberty type - loaded at London, left Thames 0600 7th, ETA Gold 8th (Convoy ETM2)

WILLIAM N. PENDLETON 7,244/43 US Liberty type - after loading, left Falmouth, ETA Utah 10th (Convoy ECM2): returned to Falmouth where arrived 1315 13th: on a subsequent voyage, unexploded bomb reported aboard 18th

WILLIAM PHIPS 7,176/43 US Liberty type - loaded at London, left Thames 0600 7th, ETA Juno 8th (Convoy ETM2): returned to London where arrived 1850 11th

WILLIAM TILGHMAN 7,191/42 US Liberty type - loaded at Southampton, left Solent, ETA Western Task Force area 9th (Convoy ECM1W)

WILLIAM TYLER PAGE 7,176/43 US Liberty type - after loading, left Avonmouth 13th, left Falmouth 1730 16th, ETA Utah 17th (Convoy ECM9)

WILLIAM W. LORING 7,176/44 US Liberty type - loaded at Southampton, left Solent, ETA Omaha 10th (Convoy ECM2W): returned to Southampton

Other Vessels, assigned for Normandy service, loading or awaiting orders in British waters during June

A. MITCHELL PALMER	7,198/44	US Liberty type	- Mersey
ABRAHAM CLARK	7,176/42	US Liberty type	- Mersey
ALBERT P. RYDER	7,176/43	US Liberty type	- Oban
ALCOA BANNER	5,035/19	US (Alcoa)	- Oban
AMERIKI	7,176/43	Greek US Liberty type	- Mersey
ARTHUR R. LEWIS	7,240/44	US Liberty type	- Mersey
AUGUSTUS SAINT-GAUDENS	7,176/44	US Liberty type	- Newport
BARTHOLOMEW GOSNOLD	7,176/43	US Liberty type	- Milford Haven
BENITO JUAREZ	7,244/43	US Liberty type	- Oban
BENJAMIN H. BRISTOW	7,191/43	US Liberty type	- Mersey
BENJAMIN HOLT	7,176/43	US Liberty type	- Newport
CAPE SABLE	4,398/36	Br (Lyle)	- London
CEFN-Y-BRYN	5,164/39	Br (Cook)	- Hull
CHARLES HENDERSON	7,176/43	US Liberty type	- Oban
CHRISTOPHER S. FLANAGAN	7,247/44	US Liberty type	- Swansea
DANIEL HIESTER	7,176/42	US Liberty type	- Mersey

EDWARD KAVANAGH	7,176/44	US Liberty type	- Oban
EDWARD ROWLAND SILL	7,181/42	US Liberty type	- Mersey
EMPIRE PLOVER	6,109/20	Br (MoWT)	- London
EPHRAIM W. BAUGHMAN	7,176/43	US Liberty type	- Belfast
FISHER AMES	7,176/42	US Liberty type	- Mersey
GEORGE A. CUSTER	7,176/42	US Liberty type	- Mersey
GLENN CURTISS	7,176/43	US Liberty type	- Mersey
HAROLD T. ANDREWS	7,176/44	US Liberty type	- Mersey
HARPAGUS	7,271/42	Br (Hain)	- Hull
HENRY MILLER	7,207/43	US Liberty type	- Oban
IGNACE PADEREWSKI	7,176/43	US Liberty type	- Oban
J. WILLARD GIBBS	7,176/43	US Liberty type	- Milford Haven
JACQUES CARTIER	7,176/43	US Liberty type	- Mersey
JAMES E. HAVILAND	7,244/43	US Liberty type	- Mersey
JOHN C. FREMONT	7,176/41	US Liberty type	- Clyde
JOHN GRIER HIBBEN	7,176/43	US Liberty type	- Mersey
JOHN L. ELLIOTT	7,210/44	US Liberty type	- Mersey

IGNACE PADEREWSKI in December 1943. [NMM P22978]

MT ships off Normandy. [IWM]

JOHN SHARP WILLIAMS	7,176/43	US Liberty type	- Milford Haven
JOSEPH W. FOLK	7,176/43	US Liberty type	- Newport
JOSHUA W. ALEXANDER	7,176/43	US Liberty type	
KING WILLIAM	5,274/28	Br (King)	- Hull
LAPLAND	2,897/42	Br (Currie)	- Mersey
MAHLON PITNEY	7,200/43	US Liberty type	- Mersey
MARYMAR	6,347/19	US	- Falmouth
NATHAN TOWSON	7,176/43	US Liberty type	- Oban
NATHANIEL BACON	7,176/42	US Liberty type	- Mersey
R. NEY McNEELY	7,198/44	US Liberty type	- Belfast
ROBERT JORDAN	7,176/43	US Liberty type	- Oban
RODSLEY	5,000/39	Br (Thomasson)	- London (Tilbury)
ROGER GRISWOLD	7,191/43	US Liberty type	- Mersey
SAMAKRON	7,219/43	Br (MoWT) US Liberty type	- London
SAMLONG	7,219/43	Br (MoWT) US Liberty type	- London (Tilbury)
SAMNEAGH	7,210/44	Br (MoWT) US Liberty type	- Hull
SAMOKLA	7,219/43	Br (MoWT) US Liberty type	- London
SAMUEL CHASE	7,191/42	US Liberty type	- Oban
TEMPLE YARD	5,205/37	Br (Temple)	- Hull
THOMAS BAILEY ALDRICH	7,176/42	US Liberty type	- Mersey
TREVELYAN	7,292/43	Br (Hain)	- Hull
WASHINGTON ALLSTON	7,176/44	US Liberty type	- Clyde
WILLIAM C. ENDICOTT	7,181/42	US Liberty type	- Mersey
WILLIAM H. PRESCOTT	7,176/42	US Liberty type	- Mersey
WILLIAM KENT	7,187/42	US Liberty type	- Cardiff
WILLIAM PEPPERELL	7,176/43	US Liberty type	- Mersey
WILLIAM THORNTON	7,176/43	US Liberty type	- Mersey
WILLIAM WINDOM	7,194/43	US Liberty type	- Oban

Section A3 - COASTERS AND SHORT SEA CARGO SHIPS
including military store ships
and cased petrol carriers.

Coasters played a vital part in Operation Neptune. [IWM]

Although most of the ships in this grouping sailed under the Red Ensign, they were truly multi-national in origin - American, Belgian, British, Canadian, Danish, Dutch, Estonian, French, Norwegian and Polish. The initial coaster convoys assembled in the Thames and Bristol Channel, moved to the Solent and from there crossed to France, a few as part of the initial assault fleet. On completion of their first round trip, most became part of a continuous sailing programme from more than twenty different loading ports, large and small, on the south coast, in the West Country and Bristol Channel, and on the Thames and east coast. After initial apprehension about the possible dangers involved, it was found that small coasters could be beached, dried out and discharged with an ease and efficiency that made them the perfect aid to a rapid stores build up.

NAME OF VESSEL   Tonnage/year of build, nationality (owner) - origin and/or assembly area, destination and convoy of first sailing: other information. (All dates are June 1944 unless otherwise stated.)

AARO   1,426/25   Br (MoWT) ex-Danish - after loading, left Swansea 3rd, left Bristol Channel 5th, ETA Omaha 8th (Convoy EBC2Z)

ABILITY   881/43   Br (Everard) - left Thames, ETA Sword 14th (Convoy ETC8)

ACTINIA   352/37   Dutch - loaded at Port Talbot, left Bristol Channel 2nd, via Solent, for Omaha (intended for Convoy EBC3W ETA 9th)

ACTIVITY   358/31   Br (Everard) - left Thames 0215 5th, via Solent, for Eastern Task Force area (intended for Convoy ETC3W ETA 9th): left for London 12th

ALACRITY   554/40   Br (Everard) - ex Thames, left Solent, ETA Sword 11th (Convoy ETC5W): returned to London where arrived 15th

ALBERT C. FIELD   1,764/23   Canadian - after loading, left Penarth 1600 16th, ETA Utah 19th (Convoy EBC14) to discharge 2,500 tons ammunition: 2340 18th hit by aerial torpedo, vessel broke in two and sank

ALGOL   1,566/24   Br (Kyle) - arrived London 25th May to load, left Thames, ETA Juno 12th (Convoy ETC6)

ALNWICK   508/36   Br (Tyne-Tees) - ex Clyde, arrived Weymouth Bay 26th May (intended for Convoy ETC22W ETA Eastern Task Force area 8th)

ANDONI   678/37   Br (Evans) - left Solent, ETA Utah 11th (Convoy EBC5W): returned to Llanelly and Sharpness

ANTHONY ENRIGHT   1,791/43   Br (MoWT) US - after loading, left Swansea 12th, left Bristol Channel, ETA Omaha 16th (Convoy EBC10)

ANTICOSTI   1,925/21   Canadian - ex London for Eastern Task Force area (intended for Convoy ETC2Z ETA 7th): returned to London where arrived 16th

ANTIQUITY   311/33   Br (Everard) - arrived London 22nd May to load, left Thames 0100 7th, ETA Sword 8th (Convoy ETC22)

ANTRIM COAST   646/37   Br (Coast Lines) - loaded at Port Talbot, left Solent, ETA Omaha 10th (Convoy EBC4W): returned to Portishead where arrived 19th

APRICITY   402/33   Br (Everard) - loaded at London, left Thames 31st May, left Solent (Anchorage 3N/c9), arrived Gold 6th (Follow-up Convoy L1)

ARA   965/19   Norwegian - loaded at Southampton, left Solent 14th, ETA Gold 15th (Convoy ETC9W)

ARBROATH   553/35   Br (Dundee, Perth & London) - ex Thames, left Solent, ETA Juno 13th (Convoy ETC7W)

ARDGRYFE   975/18   Br (MacCallum) - left Thames 0100 7th, left Solent, ETA Juno 10th (Convoy ETC4W): discharged cargo of ordnance and supplies 1600 11th-2400 12th

ASTERIA post-war. [P. Sweeney]

ARIDITY   336/31   Br (Everard) - arrived London 8th May to load, left Thames 0100 7th, ETA Gold 8th (Convoy ETC22)

ASA ELDRIDGE   1,791/43   Br (MoWT) US - arrived London 25th May to load, left Thames 0100 7th, ETA Gold 8th (Convoy ETC22): on a subsequent voyage, damaged by grounding on Calvados shoal 20th, refloated 21st and towed to Solent by tug CHEERLY 22nd for bottom damage, steering gear and boiler repairs

ASEITY   416/35   Br (Everard) - ex Thames, left Solent, ETA Juno 12th (Convoy ETC6W): returned to London where arrived 18th

ASHANTI   534/36   Br (Evans) - left Thames 0100 7th, left Solent, ETA Juno 10th (Convoy ETC4W) but sunk en route by E-boat 10th

ASHBEL HUBBARD   1,793/43   Br (MoWT) US - after loading, left Barry 9th, left Bristol Channel 10th, ETA Omaha 13th (Convoy EBC7)

ASHMUN J. CLOUGH   1,791/43   Br (MoWT) US - after loading, left Cardiff 5th, left Bristol Channel 7th, ETA Omaha 10th (Convoy EBC4)

ASK   1,541/17   Norwegian - after loading, left Newport 10th, left Bristol Channel 11th, ETA Omaha 14th (Convoy EBC8)

ASSIDUITY   350/30   Br (Everard) - left Thames 0215 5th, via Solent, for Eastern Task Force area (intended for Convoy ETC3W ETA 9th)

ASTERIA   649/26   Br (Robertson) - after loading, left London 5th, left Thames 0100 7th, left Solent, ETA Sword 10th (Convoy ETC4W)

ATLANTIC COAST   890/34   Br (Coast Lines) - after loading, left Sharpness 10th, left Bristol Channel 12th, ETA Western Task Force area 15th (Convoy EBC9)

AVANCE 1,582/20 Br (MoWT) ex-Danish - loaded at Swansea, left Bristol Channel 5th, ETA Omaha 8th (Convoy EBC2Z)

AVANCE I 1,300/12 Norwegian - loaded at Newport, left Bristol Channel, ETA Omaha 15th (Convoy EBC9): returned to Newport where arrived 20th

AVANVILLE 683/20 Br (Monks) - loaded at London, left Thames 31st May, left Solent (Anchorage 4/c5), arrived Sword 0830 7th (Convoy EWC1B): returned to Newhaven: on a subsequent voyage, damaged and beached at Sword 23rd

BAILEY FOSTER 1,791/43 Br (MoWT) US - after loading, left Barry 3rd, left Bristol Channel 6th for Western Task Force area (intended for Convoy EBC3 ETA 9th)

BALDUIN 1,164/21 Norwegian - arrived Southampton 12th to load, left Solent, ETA Gold 15th (Convoy ETC9W)

BARONSCOURT 869/35 Br (Kelly) - left Thames 0215 5th, left Solent, arrived Juno 9th (Convoy ETC3W): discharged cargo of ordnance and supplies 1900 9th-0900 11th

BEAL 504/36 Br (Tyne-Tees) - (intended for Convoy ETC4W ETA Port en Bessin 10th) returned 12th

BEECHFIELD 449/22 Br (Zillah) - after loading, left London 2nd, left Thames 0215 5th, left Solent 2100 7th, ETA Sword 8th (Convoy ETC22W): left for London 12th

BEESTON 466/21 Br (ICI) - after loading, left Avonmouth 1st, left Bristol Channel 2nd, left Solent 1900 7th, ETA Utah 8th (Convoy EBC2W): returned to Southampton

BELFORD 366/20 Br (Piggins) - after loading, left London 4th, left Thames 5th, left Solent 2100 7th, ETA Eastern Task Force area 8th (Convoy ETC22W)

BENGUELA 534/36 Br (Metcalf) - ex Thames, left Solent, ETA Gold 13th (Convoy ETC7W): returned to London where arrived 16th

BENJAMIN SHERBURN 1,814/43 Br (MoWT) US - left Thames, ETA Juno 11th (Convoy ETC5): returned to London where arrived 18th

BERRYDEN 506/04 Br (Taylor) - loaded at London, left Thames 0215 5th, left Solent 2100 7th, ETA Gold 8th (Convoy ETC22W)

BIDASSOA 558/01 Br (MoWT) ex-French - loaded at Swansea, left Bristol Channel 30th May, via Solent (Anchorage 3N/b4) (intended for Assault Force O ETA Omaha 6th): returned to Fowey (ETA 13th)

BIRKER FORCE 953/19 Br (West Coast) - arrived London 19th May to load, left Thames, ETA Juno 10th (Convoy ETC4)

BLACKTOFT 1,109/10 Br (Toft) - left Thames 0215 5th, via Solent, for Eastern Task Force area (intended for Convoy ETC3W ETA 9th): returned to London where arrived 17th

BLACKWATER 707/07 Br (Kelly) - loaded at London, left Thames 0215 5th, left Solent 2100 7th, ETA Sword 8th (Convoy ETC22W): returned to Newhaven

BONAWE 355/19 Br (Gardner) - after loading, left London 2nd, left Thames 0215 5th, left Solent 2100 7th, ETA Gold 8th (Convoy ETC22W)

BOSTON TRADER 371/36 Br (Great Yarmouth) - left Thames 0100 7th, left Solent, ETA Sword 10th (Convoy ETC4W): returned to London where arrived 13th

BRACKENFIELD 657/37 Br (Zillah) - left Thames 0100 7th, left Solent 1430 9th, ETA Juno 10th (Convoy ETC4W) to discharge 660 tons ammunition: 0310 10th hit port side aft by E-boat torpedo and sank immediately

BRAMHILL 1,834/23 Br (Hudson) - after loading, left Swansea 12th, left Bristol Channel 13th, ETA Omaha 16th (Convoy EBC10)

BREM 428/39 Dutch - ex Thames, left Solent, ETA Juno 12th (Convoy ETC6W): returned to Solent

BRIARFIELD 446/20 Br (Zillah) - loaded at Cardiff, left Solent, ETA Omaha 13th (Convoy EBC7W): returned to Southampton (Berth 105) where arrived 20th

BROCKLEY COMBE 662/38 Br (Ald) - ex Port Talbot for Western Task Force area (intended for Convoy EBC2Y ETA 8th): returned to Llanelly

BROOMFIELD 657/38 Br (Zillah) - loaded at London, left Thames 0215 5th, left Solent 2100 7th, ETA Juno 8th (Convoy ETC22W): discharged cargo of ammunition 1800 9th-1000 12th: returned to Newhaven

BROOMLANDS 518/20 Br (Chester) - after loading, left London (Tilbury) 16th May, left Thames 31st May, left Solent (Anchorage 3N/c3), arrived Juno 6th (Follow-up Convoy L1): discharged cargo of ammunition 2100 6th-0400 8th

BRYNHILD 2,195/07 Br (MoWT) ex-Danish - left Thames, ETA Gold 13th (Convoy ETC7): discharged cargo of Royal Engineers' stores 1035 14th-1330 17th

BUCKLAW 424/43 Br (Gibson) - left Thames 0100 7th, left Solent, ETA Gold 10th (Convoy ETC4W): returned to London (Purfleet A)

BUSIRIS 943/29 Br (Moss Hutchison) - loaded at Southampton, left Solent, ETA Gold 17th (Convoy ETC11W)

CAIRNGORM 394/38 Br (Robertson) - loaded at Sharpness, left Bristol Channel 2nd, via Solent, for Utah (intended for Convoy EBC3W ETA 9th): returned to Poole

CALVIN COGGIN 1,791/43 Br (MoWT) US - after loading, left Cardiff 11th, left Bristol Channel 12th, ETA Omaha 15th (Convoy EBC9)

CAMEO 946/37 Br (Robertson) - loaded at Sharpness, left Bristol Channel 30th May, via Solent (Anchorage 3N/b1) (intended for Assault Force U ETA Utah 6th)

CAIRNGORM post-war. [P. Sweeney]

CAPITO   968/18   Br (Bristol) - after loading, left Portishead 7th, left Solent 12th, ETA Utah 13th (Convoy EBC7W)

CARNALEA   619/13   Br (Barkley) - ex Thames, left Solent, ETA Gold 12th (Convoy ETC6W): returned to Southampton for repairs

CARRICK COAST   369/34   Br (Coast Lines) - loaded at Garston, left Solent, ETA Omaha 10th (Convoy EBC4W): completed discharge 16th and sailed for Southampton

CASSARD   1,602/20   Br (MoWT) ex-French - loaded at Southampton, left Solent, ETA Omaha 24th (Convoy EBC17W) to discharge 2,000 dwt tons of stores

CASTLE COMBE   454/36   Br (Ald) - loaded at Sharpness, left Solent, ETA Utah 12th (Convoy EBC6W)

CEDARWOOD   899/33   Br (Constantine) - loaded at Portishead, left Bristol Channel 2nd, via Solent, for Utah (intended for Convoy EBC3W ETA 9th): returned to Swansea

CHANNEL FISHER   700/21   Br (Fisher) - left Thames, ETA Gold 28th (Convoy ETC20) but put back to Thames 27th as unable to maintain convoy speed

CHANNEL QUEEN   567/40   Br (British Channel Islands) - ex Thames, left Solent, ETA Juno 11th (Convoy ETC5W)

CHARLES H. SALTER   1,814/42   Br (MoWT) US - left Thames, ETA Gold 10th (Convoy ETC4)

CHARLES TREADWELL   1,814/43   Br (MoWT) US - left Thames 0100 7th, via Solent, for Eastern Task Force area: returned to Bristol Channel

CHELWOOD   2,742/28   Br (France, Fenwick) - loaded at London, left Thames for Eastern Task Force area (intended for Convoy ETC2Y ETA 7th): returned to London (Berth 14, Tilbury Dock) where arrived 0730 11th: on a subsequent voyage, went aground on Calvados shoal 20th-22nd after which entered Mulberry B to discharge cargo

CHORZOW   845/21   Polish - loaded at Penarth, left Bristol Channel 2nd, left Solent 1900 7th, ETA Utah 8th (Convoy EBC2W): returned to Southampton

CIRCE II   2,031/26   Br (MoWT) ex-French - loaded at Swansea, left Bristol Channel 5th, ETA Utah 8th (Convoy EBC2Z)

CITRINE   783/39   Br (Robertson) - after loading, left Sharpness, via Avonmouth, arrived Western Task Force area 8th (Convoy EBC2Y): damaged 8th: returned to Sharpness: on the next voyage, struck submerged object off beach-head 20th and beached 22nd-24th: further damaged in collision with unknown vessel while returning to Solent 26th

CITY OF CHARLEROY   869/33   Br (Brussels SS) - ex Thames, left Solent, ETA Gold 12th (Convoy ETC6W)

CITY OF MALINES   373/05   Br (Great Yarmouth) - loaded at London, left Thames 28th for Sword but, following a collision, put into Dover for stern damage repairs 1800 28th: continued the following day

CLARA MONKS   577/20   Br (Monks) - ex Thames, left Solent, ETA Sword 11th (Convoy ETC5W)

CLAUDIUS MAGNIN   2,310/21   Br (MoWT) ex-French - loaded at Swansea, left Bristol Channel 5th, ETA Utah 8th (Convoy EBC2Z): returned to Barry

CLEMENT T. JAYNE   1,793/43   Br (MoWT) US - after loading, left Avonmouth 6th, ETA Utah 10th (Convoy EBC4)

CLERMISTON   1,498/21   Br (London & Edinburgh) - loaded at Penarth, left Bristol Channel 14th, ETA Omaha 17th (Convoy EBC12) to discharge ammunition: returned to Penarth

CORAL   638/19   Br (Robertson) - loaded at Penarth, left Bristol Channel 2nd, via Solent, for Utah (intended for Convoy EBC3W ETA 9th)

CORAL QUEEN   303/41   Br (British Channel Traders) - after loading, left Port Talbot 2nd for Western Task Force area (intended for Convoy EBC2Y ETA 8th): returned to Southampton 11th

Coasters beached for cargo discharge. [IWM]

CORBRIDGE 1,703/28 Br (Cory) - after loading, left London 10th, left Thames, ETA Gold 13th (Convoy ETC7)

CORDALE 2,143/25 Br (Cory) - after loading, left London 9th, left Thames, ETA Gold 12th (Convoy ETC6)

CORGLEN 2,822/29 Br (Cory) - loaded at London, left Thames for Eastern Task Force area (intended for Convoy ETC2Z ETA 7th): returned to Thames where arrived 10th

CORNISH COAST 219/37 Br (Coast Lines) - withdrawn end May

CORSEA 2,764/21 Br (Cory) - loaded at London, left Thames for Eastern Task Force area (intended for Convoy ETC2Y ETA 7th): returned to Thames 9th/10th

CORUNDUM 929/25 Br (Robertson) - loaded at London, left Thames 0215 5th for Solent (intended for Convoy ETC22W ETA Juno 8th): returned 14th

COXWOLD 1,124/38 Br (Yorkshire Dale) - left Bristol Channel, ETA Omaha 11th (Convoy EBC5): returned to Sharpness where arrived 20th

CRAGSIDE 496/35 Br (Tyne-Tees) - arrived London 8th May to load, left Thames 0100 7th, ETA Gold 8th (Convoy ETC22)

CRESCENDO 348/38 Dutch - after loading, left Port Talbot 2nd, left Solent, ETA Omaha 11th (Convoy EBC5W)

CRESCO 1,270/16 Norwegian - ex Thames, left Solent, ETA Sword 10th (Convoy ETC4W)

CREWHILL 695/23 Br (Kelly) - loaded at Barry, left Bristol Channel 30th May, left Solent (Anchorage 4/d2), arrived Omaha 0600 7th (Convoy EWC1A): returned to Southampton, under repair 19th

CUSHENDUN 646/04 Br (Longstaff) - loaded at Portishead, left Bristol Channel 30th May, left Solent (Anchorage 4/d4), arrived Utah 0600 7th (Convoy EWC1A): returned to Southampton

CYRUS SEARS 1,814/43 Br (MoWT) US - ex Thames, ETA Gold 10th (Convoy ETC4)

DAGENHAM 2,178/19 Br (Hudson) - loaded at London (Berth 15, Tilbury Dock), left Thames, ETA Sword 14th (Convoy ETC8): returned to London where arrived 21st

DALEWOOD 2,774/31 Br (France, Fenwick) - loaded at Swansea, left Bristol Channel 5th, ETA Utah 8th (Convoy EBC2Z)

DEEMOUNT 569/33 Br (Border) - loaded at London, left Thames 0100 7th, ETA Sword 8th (Convoy ETC22)

DENBIGH COAST 484/37 Br (Coast Lines) - loaded at Port Talbot, left Solent, ETA Omaha 13th (Convoy EBC7W): completed discharge 16th: returned to Port Talbot where arrived 19th

DICKY 507/01 Br (Culliford) - loaded at London, left Thames 0215 5th, left Solent 2100 7th, ETA Sword 8th (Convoy ETC22W): returned to Plymouth

DONA FLORA 1,179/24 Br (Kingdon) - loaded at Southampton, left Solent, ETA Utah 15th (Convoy EBC9W): rudder damaged in storm so vessel beached at Utah approx 21st

DORRIEN ROSE 1,039/22 Br (Hughes) - arrived London 15th May to load, left Solent, ETA Sword 13th (Convoy ETC7W)

DOWNLEAZE 486/24 Br (Osborn & Wallis) - ex Bristol Channel, via Solent, left Poole 17th

DOWNSHIRE 398/25 Br (East Downshire) - loaded at Newport, left Solent, ETA Omaha 11th (Convoy EBC5W)

DRAKE 531/38 Br (General Steam) - loaded at Sharpness, left Solent 9th, ETA Utah 10th (Convoy EBC4W) to discharge cased petrol

DUNGRANGE 621/14 Br (Dungrange) - after loading, left London 5th, left Thames 0100 7th, left Solent 1500 9th, ETA Juno 10th (Convoy ETC4W) to discharge ammunition: 0400 10th hit by E-boat torpedo 25 miles from French coast and sank within 3 minutes

DUNVEGAN HEAD 638/20 Br (Henry & MacGregor) - after loading, left London 30th May, left Thames 31st May, left Solent (Anchorage 4/e6), arrived Sword 0830 7th (Convoy EWC1B): on a subsequent voyage, at 2130 22nd, while ship beached at Sword and all crew sheltering ashore, vessel set ablaze by two shell hits in her cargo of ammunition, fire not extinguished until 24th

DURWARD 419/40 Br (Gibson) - loaded at London, left Thames 31st May, left Solent, arrived Gold 0830 7th (Convoy EWC1B)

EAGLESCLIFFE HALL 1,900/28 Canadian (Hall Corporation) - (intended for Eastern Task Force area) left London 1st, arrived Hull 6th

EAST COASTER 469/19 Br (British Isles) - loaded at Penarth, left Solent, ETA Utah 10th (Convoy EBC4W): returned to Plymouth where arrived 16th

EASTWOOD 1,551/24 Br (France, Fenwick) - loaded at Port Talbot, left Bristol Channel 5th, ETA Omaha 8th (Convoy EBC2Z)

EBBRIX 258/38 Br (Rix) - loaded at London, left Thames 31st May, left Solent (Anchorage 3S/a7), arrived Juno 0830 7th (Convoy EWC1B)

EDENSIDE 366/21 Br (Rose) - arrived London 7th to load for Eastern Task Force area: returned to Solent 13th

EDINA 489/39 Br (Currie) - loaded at Garston, left Solent, ETA Omaha 12th (Convoy EBC6W): returned to Llanelly where arrived 18th to load cased petrol

EDLE 654/16 Norwegian - loaded at Swansea, left Bristol Channel 30th May, via Solent (Anchorage 3N/b6) (intended for Assault Force O ETA Omaha 6th): returned to Fowey

EGEE 2,667/40 Br (MoWT) ex-French - loaded at Penarth, left Bristol Channel, ETA Omaha 23rd (Convoy EBC16)

EILDON 1,447/36 Br (Gibson) - loaded at Avonmouth, left Solent 11th, ETA Utah 12th (Convoy EBC6W)

EILIAN HILL 781/13 Br (Thomas) - ex Thames, left Solent, ETA Sword 11th (Convoy ETC5W): on a subsequent voyage, damaged at Port en Bessin 22nd

ELIDIR 398/03 Br (Coppack) - ex Thames, via Solent, for Gold (intended for Convoy ETC3W ETA 9th): returned to Southampton

ELKANAH CROWELL 1,791/43 Br (MoWT) US - loaded at Avonmouth for Western Task Force area (intended for Convoy EBC3 ETA 9th): returned to Cardiff where arrived 18th

EMPIRE BANK 402/41 Br (MoWT) - ex Thames, left Solent, ETA Gold 11th (Convoy ETC5W)

EMPIRE BOND 2,088/06 Br (MoWT) - after loading, left Cardiff 13th, ETA Utah 16th (Convoy EBC11)

EMPIRE CAPE 872/41 Br (MoWT) - loaded at Port Talbot, left Bristol Channel 30th May, via Solent (Anchorage 3N/b1) (intended for Assault Force O ETA Omaha 6th): returned to Portishead where arrived 16th

EMPIRE CLIFF 873/40 Br (MoWT) - loaded at Garston, left Solent, ETA Omaha 13th (Convoy EBC7W)

EMPIRE CREEK 332/41 Br (MoWT) - after loading, left Plymouth 0432 16th, ETA Utah 17th (Convoy EBC12) to discharge 384 dwt tons of cased petrol: returned to Plymouth

EMPIRE ESTUARY 319/40 Br (MoWT) - after loading, left Port Talbot 1st, left Bristol Channel 2nd, via Solent, for Omaha (intended for Convoy EBC3W ETA 9th)

EMPIRE FORELAND 873/41 Br (MoWT) - loaded at Garston, left Solent, ETA Omaha 13th (Convoy EBC7W)

EMPIRE HEARTH 2,020/42 Br (MoWT) - ex London for Eastern Task Force area (intended for Convoy ETC2Z ETA 7th): returned to Thames where arrived 13th

EMPIRE JONQUIL 369/39 Br (MoWT) - loaded at Port Talbot, left Bristol Channel 2nd, via Solent, for Omaha (intended for Convoy EBC3W ETA 9th)

EMPIRE LAGOON 2,013/41 Br (MoWT) - ex London for Eastern Task Force area (intended for Convoy ETC2Z ETA 7th): returned to Thames where arrived 10th

EMPIRE LOUGH 2,824/40 Br (MoWT) - ex London for Eastern Task Force area (intended for Convoy ETC2Z ETA 7th): returned to London where arrived 10th: on a subsequent voyage, at 1520 24th, while carrying 2,800 tons cased petrol for Gold, vessel set ablaze by two shell hits in Strait of Dover: beached by tug LADY BRASSEY west of Dover 24th, still on fire 26th

EMPIRE NESS 2,922/41 Br (MoWT) - ex London for Eastern Task Force area (intended for Convoy ETC2Z ETA 7th)

EMPIRE NUTFIELD 1,561/19 Br (MoWT) - after loading, left London 3rd, left Thames 5th for Eastern Task Force area (intended for Convoy ETC2Z ETA 7th): returned 9th

EMPIRE RESISTANCE 1,631/08 Br (MoWT) - after loading, left Newport 11th, left Bristol Channel 12th, ETA Omaha 15th (Convoy EBC9)

EMPIRE RIDER 965/43 Br (MoWT) - after loading, left London 15th, left Thames, ETA Juno 17th (Convoy ETC11)

EMPIRE SCOUT 2,229/36 Br (MoWT) - after loading, left Port Talbot 12th, left Bristol Channel 13th, ETA Omaha 16th (Convoy EBC10)

EMPIRE SEAMAN 2,905/43 Br (MoWT) - left Tyne 16th, anchored Thames 18th, left 28th, ETA Mulberry B 29th (Convoy ETC21)

EMPIRE SEDGE 2,852/41 Br (MoWT) - loaded at Swansea, left Bristol Channel 5th, ETA Omaha 8th (Convoy EBC2Z): returned to Swansea

EMPIRE SHOAL 878/41   Br (MoWT) - loaded at Sharpness, left Solent, ETA Omaha 10th (Convoy EBC4W): returned to Portishead where arrived 19th

EMPIRE STRAIT 2,824/40   Br (MoWT) - loaded at Swansea, left Bristol Channel 5th, ETA Omaha 8th (Convoy EBC2Z): returned to Grimsby where arrived 15th

ENID MARY 582/21   Br (British Isles) - after loading, left London 30th May, left Thames 31st May, left Solent (Anchorage 4/c2), arrived Juno 0830 7th (Convoy EWC1B)

ERICA 1,592/19   Norwegian - loaded at Swansea, left Bristol Channel 5th, ETA Omaha 8th (Convoy EBC2Z)

ERNA 361/40   Dutch - loaded at Port Talbot, left Bristol Channel 30th May, left Solent (Anchorage 4/e1), arrived Omaha 0600 7th (Convoy EWC1A)

ESKWOOD 791/11   Br (Grand Union) - left Thames 0215 5th, via Solent, for Eastern Task Force area (intended for Convoy ETC3W ETA 9th): returned to Solent 14th

EUTERPE 897/03   Dutch - loaded at Southampton, left Solent, ETA Gold 28th (Convoy ETC20W)

EVERTSEN 392/29   Dutch - ex Bristol Channel, via Poole, left Solent, ETA Gold 15th (Convoy ETC9W)

FAGERBRO 994/23   Norwegian - after loading, left Southampton 12th, left Solent 14th, ETA Utah 15th (Convoy EBC9W)

FANO 1,889/22   Br (MoWT) ex-Danish - loaded at Swansea, left Bristol Channel 5th, ETA Omaha 8th (Convoy EBC2Z): returned to Swansea

FENJA 847/24   Br (South Georgia) - left Thames, ETA Sword 14th (Convoy ETC8)

FIRE QUEEN 650/21   Br (Coast Lines) - loaded at Newport, left Solent, ETA Omaha 10th (Convoy EBC4W): returned to Southampton

FAGERBRO (left) beached in the Western Task Force area. [IWM KY30224]

FLATHOUSE, the first coaster to unload inside Mulberry B. [IWM A24087]

FLATHOUSE   1,546/31   Br (Stephenson Clarke) - left Thames 0100 7th, left Solent, ETA Gold 10th (Convoy ETC4W): returned to London (Tilbury)

FLUOR   914/25   Br (Robertson) - after loading, left Avonmouth 30th May, arrived Solent (Anchorage 4/d7) 1st, for Western Task Force area (intended for Convoy EWC1A ETA 7th): returned to Southampton where started to load ammunition 1900 18th

FOLDA   1,165/20   Br (South Georgia) - after loading, left London 10th, left Thames, ETA Gold 13th (Convoy ETC7): en route collided with and sank REIAS 13th

FORELAND   1,870/39   Br (Shipping & Coal) - left Thames 0215 5th, via Solent, for Eastern Task Force area (intended for Convoy ETC3W ETA 9th): returned from Sword to London where arrived 17th

FREEMAN HATCH   1,793/43   Br (MoWT) US - after loading, left Barry 9th, left Bristol Channel, ETA Omaha 14th (Convoy EBC8)

FYLLA   792/06   Br (MoWT) ex-Danish - ex Swansea for Western Task Force area (intended for Convoy EBC2Y ETA 8th)

GALACUM   585/15   Br (Derwent) - after loading, left London 30th May, left Thames 31st May, left Solent (Anchorage 4/d8), arrived Gold 0830 7th (Convoy EWC1B): damaged 7th

GARESFIELD   2,168/24   Br (Consett) - ex London for Eastern Task Force area (intended for Convoy ETC2Z ETA 7th): returned to London where arrived 15th

GASTON MICARD   982/17   Norwegian - after loading, left Fowey, ETA Omaha 29th (Convoy EBC24)

GATESHEAD   744/19   Br (Tyne-Tees) - loaded at London, left Thames 0100 7th, ETA Sword 8th (Convoy ETC22): returned to Plymouth

GEM   640/24   Br (Robertson) - after loading, left Portishead 30th May, arrived Solent (Anchorage 4/d3) 1st, left, arrived Utah 0600 7th (Convoy EWC1A): returned to Southampton

GIRONDE   1,770/20   Belgian - after loading, left Avonmouth 9th, left Bristol Channel 10th, ETA Utah 13th (Convoy EBC7)

GLADONIA   360/39   Br (Wharton) - after loading, left London 30th May, left Thames 31st May, left Solent (Anchorage 3S/a8), arrived Sword 0830 7th (Convoy EWC1B)

GLAMIS   555/36   Br (Dundee, Perth & London) - loaded at London, left Thames 0100 7th, ETA Juno 8th (Convoy ETC22): discharged cased petrol 1200 9th-1000 11th

GLANTON   2,822/29   Br (Sharp) - loaded at Swansea, left Bristol Channel 5th, ETA Omaha 8th (Convoy EBC2Z): returned, via London, to Grimsby

GLEN   471/35   Br (Tyne-Tees) - arrived London 19th May to load, left Thames, ETA Port en Bessin 10th (Convoy ETC4)

GLEN GAIRN   904/22   Br (Brook) - after loading, left London 11th, left Thames, ETA Gold 14th (Convoy ETC8)

GLENDINNING   1,927/21   Br (Gibson) - ex London for Eastern Task Force area (intended for Convoy ETC2Z ETA 7th): returned 9th

GLENGARRIFF   868/36   Br (Kelly) - loaded at London, left Thames 31st May, left Solent (Anchorage 3N/c4), arrived Sword 6th (Follow-up Convoy L1): returned to London (Tilbury Jetty B) where arrived 10th: on a subsequent voyage, turned back to Thames with defects 26th

GOLDFINCH   454/37   Br (General Steam) - left Milford Haven 8th, via Plymouth, ETA Utah 12th (Convoy ECM4) to discharge cased petrol

GRANBY   2,051/22   Canadian - ex London for Eastern Task Force area (intended for Convoy ETC2Z ETA 7th): returned to Thames where arrived 10th

GRANFOSS   1,461/13   Norwegian - after loading, left Barry 8th, left Bristol Channel 9th, ETA Omaha 12th (Convoy EBC6)

GRANGETOFT   975/20   Br (Toft) - loaded at Portishead, left Solent 11th, ETA Utah 12th (Convoy EBC6W): on a subsequent voyage, ship's bottom damaged in storm so vessel beached at Utah 21st

GRASLIN   2,323/24   Br (MoWT) ex-French - after loading, left Swansea 3rd, left Bristol Channel 5th, ETA Utah 8th (Convoy EBC2Z)

GRENAA   1,262/17   Br (MoWT) ex-Danish - loaded at Newport, left Bristol Channel 9th, ETA Omaha 12th (Convoy EBC6)

GRETA FORCE   914/28   Br (West Coast) - loaded at Cardiff, left Solent, ETA Omaha 10th (Convoy EBC4W)

GREYFRIARS   1,142/23   Br (Newbigin) - loaded at Southampton, left Solent, ETA Omaha 23rd (Convoy EBC16W) to discharge 1,200 dwt tons of ammunition

GUDRUN MAERSK   2,294/37   Br (MoWT) ex-Danish - after loading, left Port Talbot 14th, left Bristol Channel 16th, ETA Omaha 18th (Convoy EBC13) to discharge cased petrol: returned to Swansea

GUERNSEY QUEEN   567/39   Br (British Channel Islands) - ex Thames, left Solent, ETA Sword 12th (Convoy ETC6W)

GUN   670/18   Norwegian - loaded at Penarth, left Bristol Channel 2nd, via Solent, for Utah (intended for Convoy EBC3W ETA 9th)

GURDEN GATES   1,791/43   Br (MoWT) US - left Thames, ETA Sword 11th (Convoy ETC5): returned to London (Berth 18, Tilbury Dock): on a subsequent voyage, en route to beach-head, damaged by gunfire in Strait of Dover and diverted to Solent 24th

GWENTHILLS   868/37   Br (British Channel Traders) - ex London for Eastern Task Force area (intended for Convoy ETC2Y ETA 7th)

HAARLEM   970/17   Br (Strubin) - arrived London 3rd but did not sail as planned: left Thames, ETA Juno 27th (Convoy ETC19)

HALO   2,365/19   Br (Gas Light & Coke) - left Thames, ETA Gold 11th (Convoy ETC5): returned to Grimsby where arrived 19th

HARPTREE COMBE   439/12   Br (Ohlson) - loaded at Penarth, left Solent, ETA Utah 11th (Convoy EBC5W): returned to Plymouth

HAWARDEN BRIDGE   297/40   Br (Summers) - after loading, left Sharpness 30th May, arrived Solent (Anchorage 4/e2) 1st, left, arrived Utah 0600 7th (Convoy EWC1A)

HEIEN   995/26   Norwegian - loaded at Penarth, left Bristol Channel 30th May, via Solent (Anchorage 3N/b9) (intended for Assault Force U ETA Utah 6th): returned to Swansea 11th

HEIRE   807/17   Norwegian - left Thames, arrived Juno 12th (Convoy ETC6): discharged cargo of ammunition 1130 12th-1300 14th

HELDER   979/20   Br (Williamstown) - after loading, left Portishead 8th, left Bristol Channel 9th, ETA Utah 12th (Convoy EBC6)

HEIEN being unloaded in the Western Task Force area. [IWM ZZZ12674E]

HELMOND   983/21   Br (Strubin) - after loading, left Newport 8th, left Bristol Channel 11th, ETA Omaha 14th (Convoy EBC8)

HENRI GERLINGER   1,219/06   Belgian - after loading, left Barry 2nd, left Bristol Channel 9th, ETA Utah 12th (Convoy EBC6)

HERBERT W. WALKER   365/21   Br (Wilson) - loaded at London, left Thames 0100 7th, left Solent, ETA Gold 10th (Convoy ETC4W): returned to Littlehampton

HETTON   2,714/24   Br (Hudson) - after loading, left London (Berth 17, Tilbury Dock) 11th, left Thames, ETA Gold 14th (Convoy ETC8)

HIGHWEAR   1,173/36   Br (High Hook) - after loading, left Newport 8th, left Bristol Channel 9th, ETA Omaha 12th (Convoy EBC6)

HILDUR I   1,497/19   Norwegian - after loading, left Sharpness 10th, left Bristol Channel 12th, ETA Omaha 15th (Convoy EBC9)

HOLBURN HEAD 489/25 Br (Henry & MacGregor) - loaded at London, left Thames 31st May, left Solent (Anchorage 4/c8), arrived Sword 0830 7th (Convoy EWC1B)

HOVE 435/13 Br (Coppack) - loaded at Southampton, left Solent, ETA Gold 13th (Convoy ETC7W)

IPSWICH TRADER 484/22 Br (Horlock's) - after loading, left London 30th May, left Thames 31st May, left Solent (Anchorage 4/e5), arrived Gold 0830 7th (Convoy EWC1B)

ISAC 2,385/26 Br (MoWT) ex-French - loaded at Port Talbot, left Bristol Channel 5th, ETA Omaha 8th (Convoy EBC2Z)

ISBJORN 579/07 Norwegian - loaded at Newport, left Solent 12th, ETA Omaha 13th (Convoy EBC7W): returned to Newhaven

J. F. V. 515/09 Br (Tom) - loaded at Southampton, left Solent, ETA Juno 16th (Convoy ETC10W): returned to Solent

JADE 930/38 Br (Robertson) - loaded at Port Talbot, left Solent, ETA Omaha 11th (Convoy EBC5W): returned to Sharpness

JAN BRONS 400/39 Dutch - loaded at Poole, left Solent, ETA Utah 26th (Convoy EBC21W): returned to Poole

JARGOON 691/26 Br (Robertson) - loaded at Swansea, left Bristol Channel 2nd, left Solent 1900 7th, ETA Omaha 8th (Convoy EBC2W)

JELLICOE ROSE 1,118/20 Br (Hughes) - arrived London 27th May to load, left Thames 0100 7th, ETA Gold 8th (Convoy ETC22)

JERNFJELD 1,369/17 Norwegian - after loading, left Newport 10th, left Bristol Channel 11th, ETA Utah 14th (Convoy EBC8): storm damaged and beached at Utah approx 21st

JERNLAND 1,289/05 Norwegian - after loading, left London 4th, left Thames for Eastern Task Force area (intended for Convoy ETC2Z ETA 7th): returned 9th

JESSE G. COTTING 1,791/43 Br (MoWT) US - ex Barry for Western Task Force area (intended for Convoy EBC2Y ETA 8th): returned to Cardiff where arrived 18th

JIM 833/08 Br (Strubin) - after loading, left London 7th, left Solent, ETA Juno 13th (Convoy ETC7W): returned to Solent

JOFFRE ROSE 715/15 Br (Hughes) - loaded at Avonmouth, left Bristol Channel 2nd, left Solent 1900 7th, ETA Utah 8th (Convoy EBC2W)

JOSEWYN 1,926/19 Br (Dillwyn) - loaded at Swansea, left Bristol Channel 5th, ETA Omaha 8th (Convoy EBC2Z): returned to Swansea

JOSIAH P. CRESSEY 1,791/43 Br (MoWT) US - after loading, left Barry 3rd, left Bristol Channel 5th for Western Task Force area (intended for Convoy EBC2Y ETA 8th): returned to Southampton

JULIA 549/07 Belgian - loaded at Swansea, left Bristol Channel 5th for Western Task Force area (intended for Convoy EBC2Y ETA 8th)

JUNE 400/38 Dutch - loaded at Southampton, left Solent 14th, ETA Utah 15th (Convoy EBC9W)

JUSTIN DOANE 1,791/43 Br (MoWT) US - after loading, left Avonmouth 7th, left Bristol Channel 8th, ETA Utah 11th (Convoy EBC5)

JUTA 1,559/08 Br (MoWT) ex-Estonian - loaded at Swansea, left Bristol Channel 5th, ETA Omaha 8th (Convoy EBC2Z): returned to Newport where arrived 18th

KAIDA 510/02 Br (MoWT) ex-Estonian - loaded at London, left Thames 0215 5th, left Solent 2100 7th, ETA Juno 8th (Convoy ETC22W): returned, via Portland where delayed, to Plymouth where arrived 18th to load cased petrol

KALEV 1,867/17 Br (MoWT) ex-Estonian - after loading, left Barry 7th, left Bristol Channel 8th, ETA Omaha 11th (Convoy EBC5)

KNOWLTON [IWM A20698]

KATOWICE 1,995/25 Polish - loaded at Swansea, left Bristol Channel 5th, ETA Omaha 8th (Convoy EBC2Z): returned to Penarth

KATWIJK 1,589/21 Dutch - after loading, left Barry 14th, left Bristol Channel 16th, ETA Omaha 19th (Convoy EBC14)

KENRIX 692/21 Br (Rix) - loaded at London, left Thames 31st May, left Solent (Anchorage 4/c7), arrived Juno 0830 7th (Convoy EWC1B)

KENTISH COAST 459/38 Br (Coast Lines) - loaded at Sharpness, left Solent, ETA Utah 12th (Convoy EBC6W)

KEYNOR 1,806/14 Canadian - ex London for Eastern Task Force area (intended for Convoy ETC2Z ETA 7th): returned to London (Berth 13, Tilbury Dock) where arrived 10th

KIMBALL HARLOW 1,793/42 Br (MoWT) US - loaded at Barry, left Bristol Channel, ETA Omaha 11th (Convoy EBC5): returned to Southampton

KMICIC 1,894/23 Polish - loaded at Port Talbot, left Bristol Channel 5th, ETA Omaha 8th (Convoy EBC2Z): returned to Newport

KNOWLTON 2,068/22 Canadian - ex London for Eastern Task Force area (intended for Convoy ETC2Z ETA 7th): returned to London (Berth 11, Tilbury Dock) where arrived 10th

KOLSDAL 1,269/20 Norwegian - after loading, left Newport 9th, left Bristol Channel 10th, ETA Omaha 13th (Convoy EBC7)

KONGSHAVN 751/06 Norwegian - after loading, left London 6th, left Solent, ETA Sword 11th (Convoy ETC5W): returned to Newhaven

KORDECKI 1,975/30 Polish - loaded at Swansea, left Bristol Channel 5th, ETA Utah 8th (Convoy EBC2Z): returned to Newport where arrived 18th

KRAKOW 2,017/26 Polish - loaded at Swansea, left Bristol Channel 5th, ETA Omaha 8th (Convoy EBC2Z): returned to Cardiff

KUL   1,310/07   Norwegian - left Thames 0215 5th, via Solent, for Eastern Task Force area (intended for Convoy ETC3W ETA 9th): returned to London (Tilbury Jetty A) 18th

KYLE CASTLE   845/19   Br (Walton) - loaded at London, left Thames 31st May, left Solent (Anchorage 3S/a3), arrived Gold 0830 7th (Convoy EWC1B)

KYLE QUEEN   616/13   Br (Walton) - after loading, left London 1st, left Solent (Anchorage 4/c3), arrived Juno 0830 7th (Convoy EWC1B): under repair at Southampton 19th

KYLEBANK   969/25   Br (Kyle) - loaded at Barry, left Solent, ETA Omaha 10th (Convoy EBC4W): returned to Plymouth for repairs and to load

KYLEGORM   622/14   Br (Walton) - after loading, left London 30th May, left Thames 31st May, left Solent (Anchorage 4/c6), arrived Sword 0830 7th (Convoy EWC1B): on a subsequent voyage, kept afloat off Gold by SEA SALVOR 22nd

KYLOE   2,820/30   Br (Sharp) - loaded at Swansea, left Bristol Channel 5th, ETA Omaha 8th (Convoy EBC2Z): returned to Barry

LABAN HOWES   1,793/43   Br (MoWT) US - loaded at Avonmouth, left Bristol Channel, ETA Utah 12th (Convoy EBC6): returned to Barry where arrived 19th

LADY THOMAS   294/20   Br (Thomas) - withdrawn end May

LAMBTONIAN   2,781/42   Br (Tanfield) - ex London for Eastern Task Force area (intended for Convoy ETC2Y ETA 7th): returned to Thames 9th/10th

LARCHFIELD   493/41   Br (Zillah) - loaded at Newport, left Solent, ETA Omaha 13th (Convoy EBC7W): returned to Southampton

LEKA   1,599/22   Norwegian - after loading, left Barry 9th, left Bristol Channel 11th, ETA Omaha 14th (Convoy EBC8)

LEOVILLE   1,050/22   Br (MoWT) ex-French - loaded at London, left Thames 31st May, left Solent (Anchorage 3S/a4), arrived Gold 0830 7th (Convoy EWC1B): under repair at Southampton 19th

LILIAN I   1,271/24   Br (MoWT) ex-Danish - left Bristol Channel, ETA Omaha 10th (Convoy EBC4): returned to Penarth

LILLEAA   921/22   Br (MoWT) ex-Danish - left Sharpness 2nd, left Plymouth 5th for Western Task Force area: returned to Fowey where arrived 15th

LOANDA   534/36   Br (Evans) - ex Garston for Western Task Force area (intended for Convoy EBC2Y ETA 8th)

LOTTIE R.   972/37   Br (S & R) - loaded at Port Talbot, left Bristol Channel 30th May, via Solent (Anchorage 3N/b9) (intended for Assault Force O ETA Omaha 6th): returned to Port Talbot 11th

LOWESTOFT TRADER   311/34   Br (Great Yarmouth) - loaded at Southampton, left Solent, ETA Gold 12th (Convoy ETC6) to discharge cased petrol

LYSAKER V   1,571/36   Norwegian - arrived London 9th to load, left Thames, ETA Gold 13th (Convoy ETC7)

LYSLAND   1,335/07   Norwegian - loaded at Swansea, left Bristol Channel 5th, ETA Omaha 8th (Convoy EBC2Z): returned to Swansea

MACVILLE   666/15   Br (Western) - started loading at Southampton 20th, left Solent, ETA Omaha 24th (Convoy EBC17W) to discharge ammunition

MAJORCA   1,126/21   Br (Currie) - loaded at Penarth, left Bristol Channel, ETA Utah 10th (Convoy EBC4): returned to Swansea where arrived 18th to load ammunition

MAKEFJELL   1,567/32   Norwegian - after loading, left Port Talbot 8th, left Bristol Channel 9th, ETA Omaha 12th (Convoy EBC6)

MAMMY   1,656/11   Norwegian - after loading, left Portishead 5th, left Bristol Channel 6th for Western Task Force area (intended for Convoy EBC3 ETA 9th)

MAPLEFIELD 492/41 Br (Zillah) - ex Thames, left Solent, ETA Gold 13th (Convoy ETC7W): returned to Solent

MARCEL 543/38 Belgian - loaded at London, left Thames 31st May, left Solent (Anchorage 3N/d11), arrived Sword 6th (Follow-up Convoy L1): returned to Thames 9th/10th

MARGA 1,583/23 Norwegian - after loading, left London 26th May, left Thames, ETA Gold 12th (Convoy ETC6): returned, via Solent, to Port Talbot

MARI 563/20-25 Norwegian - loaded at Swansea, left Bristol Channel 30th May, via Solent (Anchorage 3N/b3) (intended for Assault Force O ETA Omaha 6th): returned to Fowey

MARIANNE II 1,239/24 Br (MoWT) ex-Danish - ex Plymouth, after loading, left Fowey, ETA Omaha 25th (Convoy EBC20)

MARIE 1,409/24 Belgian - loaded at Sharpness, left Bristol Channel 12th, ETA Utah 15th (Convoy EBC9)

MARIE-FLORE 545/37 Belgian - left Solent, ETA Gold 15th (Convoy ETC9W): returned to Solent

MARSDEN 2,874/24 Br (Springfjord) - after loading, left Port Talbot 16th, ETA Omaha 19th (Convoy EBC14) to discharge 2,360 dwt tons of stores

MARSWORTH 366/25 Br (Grand Union) - loaded at Cardiff, left Solent 12th, ETA Omaha 13th (Convoy EBC7W)

MARX 1,259/24 Br (MoWT) ex-Danish - arrived Penarth 10th to load, left Bristol Channel 16th, ETA Utah 19th (Convoy EBC14) to discharge 1,600 dwt tons of ammunition: returned to Penarth

MAURICE ROSE 1,600/30 Br (Hughes) - arrived London 18th to load, left 23rd, left Thames 24th for Eastern Task Force area

MELISSA 520/08 Br (Alexander King) - left Plymouth 2009 12th, via Littlehampton, ETA Gold 18th (Convoy ETC12)

MELITO 1,070/15 Br (Bristol) - ex London for Eastern Task Force area (intended for Convoy ETC2Y ETA 7th): returned 15th/16th

MR. THERM 2,974/36 Br (Gas Light & Coke) - ex London for Eastern Task Force area (intended for Convoy ETC2Y ETA 7th): returned to Thames where arrived 10th

MOELFRE ROSE 631/31 Br (Hughes) - loaded at Swansea, left Bristol Channel 30th May, left Solent (Anchorage 4/d1), arrived Omaha 0600 7th (Convoy EWC1A): returned to Southampton

MONKSTONE 867/23 Br (Grace) - loaded at London, left Thames 31st May, left Solent (Anchorage 3N/c7), arrived Sword 6th (Follow-up Convoy L1)

MONKSTONE post-war. [Capt J. F. van Puyvelde]

MONKSVILLE 499/21 Br (Monks) - loaded at Swansea, left Bristol Channel 2nd, left Solent 1900 7th, ETA Omaha 8th (Convoy EBC2W): returned to Fowey where arrived 2245 12th

MOORLANDS 420/21 Br (Taylor) - after loading, left London 2nd, left Thames 0215 5th, left Solent 2100 7th, ETA Juno 8th (Convoy ETC22W)

MOSES GAY 1,791/43 Br (MoWT) US - loaded at Avonmouth, left Bristol Channel, ETA Utah 11th (Convoy EBC5): returned, via Solent, to Grimsby

MUNIN 1,285/99 Norwegian - loaded at Newport, left Bristol Channel, ETA Omaha 10th (Convoy EBC4): returned to Barry where arrived 20th

NAROCZ 1,795/15 Polish - arrived Cardiff 20th to load, left Bristol Channel, ETA Western Task Force area 26th (Convoy EBC21)

NATO 399/39 Dutch - loaded at Sharpness, left Solent 12th, ETA Utah 13th (Convoy EBC7W)

NAVIEDALE 383/06 Br (Couper) - after loading, left London 3rd, left Thames 0215 5th, left Solent 2100 7th, ETA Juno 8th (Convoy ETC22W): returned to Littlehampton

NEPHRITE 927/27 Br (Stephenson Clarke) - loaded at London, left Thames 0215 5th, left Solent 2100 7th, ETA Juno 8th (Convoy ETC22W): returned to Southampton where started to load stores 1330 19th

NESTTUN 1,271/17 Norwegian - after loading, left Penarth 11th, left Bristol Channel 13th, ETA Omaha 16th (Convoy EBC10): after hold flooded by mine explosion, vessel beached at Omaha 23rd and cargo of ammunition discharged

NEWLANDS 1,556/21 Br (Tulley) - loaded at Swansea, left Bristol Channel 5th, ETA Omaha 8th (Convoy EBC2Z): returned to Penarth where arrived 18th

NIVERNAIS 390/33 Br (MoWT) ex-French - after loading, left London 3rd, left Thames 0215 5th, via Solent, for Eastern Task Force area (intended for Convoy ETC3W ETA 9th): returned 12th

NJORD 374/39 Dutch - loaded at Newport, left Solent 12th, ETA Omaha 13th (Convoy EBC7W): returned to Solent

NORMANDY COAST 1,428/16 Br (Coast Lines) - after loading, left Sharpness, via Avonmouth, arrived Solent 8th, left, ETA Utah 11th (Convoy EBC5W)

NORTHGATE 429/41 Br (Hull Gates) - loaded at London, left Thames 31st May, left Solent (Anchorage 3N/e10), arrived Gold 6th (Follow-up Convoy L1)

NUGGET 515/13 Br (Robertson) - loaded at Avonmouth, left Solent, ETA Utah 12th (Convoy EBC6W): returned to Southampton (Berth 104/5) where arrived 20th

OBSIDIAN 811/22 Br (Robertson) - ex Cardiff for Western Task Force area (intended for Convoy EBC2Y ETA 8th): returned, via Solent where delayed, to Plymouth

OCEAN COAST 1,173/35 Br (Coast Lines) - after loading, left Port Talbot 12th, left Bristol Channel, ETA Utah 16th (Convoy EBC10): returned to Port Talbot

OLEV 1,373/09 Br (MoWT) ex-Estonian - ex London for Eastern Task Force area (intended for Convoy ETC2Y ETA 7th): returned to London where arrived 13th

OOSTERHAVEN 320/41 Dutch - left London 12th, via Littlehampton, ETA Juno 17th (Convoy ETC11W): returned to Littlehampton

ORANMORE 495/95 Br (Kelly) - loaded at Garston, left Solent, ETA Utah 10th (Convoy EBC4W)

ORIOLE 489/39 Br (General Steam) - loaded at Sharpness, left Bristol Channel 2nd, left Solent, ETA Utah 9th (Convoy EBC3W) to discharge cased petrol

ORTOLAN 489/20 Br (General Steam) - left Thames 0100 7th, left Solent, ETA Gold 11th (Convoy ETC5W) to discharge cased petrol

OXFORD 1,893/23 Canadian - ex London for Eastern Task Force area (intended for Convoy ETC2Y ETA 7th): returned to London

PALACIO 1,346/27 Br (MacAndrews) - after loading, left Sharpness 15th, ETA Utah 18th (Convoy EBC13): returned to Sharpness

PARKNASILLA 846/32 Br (Kelly) - loaded at Port Talbot, left Bristol Channel 2nd, via Solent, for Omaha (intended for Convoy EBC3W ETA 9th): returned to Llanelly

PARKWOOD 1,049/33 Br (Constantine) - loaded at Penarth, left Solent, ETA Utah 11th (Convoy EBC5W): returned to Swansea

PAUL EMILE JAVARY 2,471/26 Br (MoWT) ex-French - after loading, left Port Talbot 13th, ETA Omaha 16th (Convoy EBC11)

PEBBLE 597/25 Br (Robertson) - loaded at Swansea, left Bristol Channel 2nd, left Solent 1900 7th, ETA Omaha 8th (Convoy EBC2W): returned to Southampton

PLASMA 325/99 Br (Sheves) - late withdrawal from Convoy EWC1B for repairs at London (Berth 3, Tilbury Dock): sailed for beach-head, ETA 25th

POLGLEN 795/15 Br (Strubin) - loaded at London, left Thames 31st May, left Solent (Anchorage 3N/c5), arrived Gold 6th (Follow-up Convoy L1): returned to Avonmouth where arrived 16th

POLLY M. 380/37 Br (Metcalf) - loaded at London, left Thames 0215 5th, via Solent, for Eastern Task Force area (intended for Convoy ETC3W ETA 9th): returned 12th

PORTHREPTA 643/22 Br (Care) - loaded at Avonmouth, left Bristol Channel 2nd, via Solent, for Utah (intended for Convoy EBC3W ETA 9th)

PORTIA 801/25 Br (Coast Lines) - loaded at Barry, left Solent, ETA Omaha 10th (Convoy EBC4W)

POZNAN 2,017/26 Polish - loaded at Penarth, left Bristol Channel 15th, ETA Omaha 18th (Convoy EBC13) to discharge ammunition

PRASE 374/38 Br (Robertson) - loaded at Port Talbot, left Solent, ETA Omaha 11th (Convoy EBC5W)

QUENTIN 500/40 Br (Gibson) - ex Port Talbot for Western Task Force area (intended for Convoy EBC2Y ETA 8th)

RAFTSUND 610/19 Norwegian - loaded at Portishead, left Solent, ETA Utah 11th (Convoy EBC5W): returned to Swansea

REDCAR 1,475/20 Br (P & O) - ex London for Eastern Task Force area (intended for Convoy ETC2Z ETA 7th): returned to London (Berth 10, Tilbury Dock) 10th

REGFOS 1,548/10 Br (Tyne & Wear) - after loading, left London 3rd, left Thames 5th for Juno (intended for Convoy ETC2Y ETA 7th): damaged at Juno 8th

REIAS 1,128/18 Norwegian - after loading, left London 4th, left Thames 5th for Eastern Task Force area (intended for Convoy ETC2Z ETA 7th): sunk in collision with FOLDA 13th

REUBEN SNOW 1,813/43 Br (MoWT) US - loaded at Avonmouth, left Bristol Channel 2nd, via Solent, for Utah (intended for Convoy EBC3W ETA 9th): returned to Barry where arrived 18th

RICHARD BEARSE 1,791/42 Br (MoWT) US - left Thames, ETA Gold 13th (Convoy ETC7)

RINGEN 1,499/17 Norwegian - left Thames 0215 5th, via Solent, for Eastern Task Force area (intended for Convoy ETC3W ETA 9th): returned 14th

ROCKLEAZE 486/24 Br (Osborn & Wallis) - loaded at Swansea, left Bristol Channel 30th May, left Solent (Anchorage 4/e3), arrived Omaha 0600 7th (Convoy EWC1A) to discharge cargo of ammunition: returned to Southampton

ROCKVILLE 481/22 Br (Monks) - after loading, left London 3rd, left Solent, arrived Sword 0830 7th (Convoy EWC1B)

RONAN post-war. [A. Duncan]

RODNEY BAXTER 1,791/42 Br (MoWT) US - loaded at Penarth, left Bristol Channel, ETA Utah 25th (Convoy EBC20) to discharge 1,939 dwt tons of ammunition

RONAN 1,489/38 Br (Gibson) - after loading, left London 20th May, left Thames, ETA Gold 11th (Convoy ETC5): returned, via Solent, to Port Talbot

RONDO 2,750/27 Br (Pelton) - after loading, left Cardiff 2nd, left Bristol Channel 5th for Western Task Force area (intended for Convoy EBC2Y ETA 8th): considerably damaged by landing craft 20th

ROSEMARIE 400/39 Dutch - loaded at London, left Thames, ETA Port en Bessin 12th (Convoy ETC6): returned to Southampton

ROWANFIELD 495/38 Br (Zillah) - ex Thames, left Solent, ETA Sword 13th (Convoy ETC7W): returned to Poole

ROYAL 759/18 Norwegian - ex Cardiff for Western Task Force area (intended for Convoy EBC2Y ETA 8th)

RUNNELSTONE 869/23 Br (S & R) - left Thames 0215 5th, via Solent, for Eastern Task Force area (intended for Convoy ETC3W ETA 9th): returned 14th/15th

S. N. A. 8 2,569/30 Br (MoWT) ex-French - after loading, left London 10th, left Thames, ETA Gold 13th (Convoy ETC7)

S. N. A. 10 2,921/20 Br (MoWT) ex-French - loaded at Newport, left Bristol Channel, ETA Omaha 25th (Convoy EBC20) to discharge 3,766 dwt tons of ammunition

SAINT ANGUS 391/36 Br (Gardner) - after loading, left London 23rd May, left Thames, left Solent, ETA Gold 11th (Convoy ETC5W)

SAINT BEDAN 452/37 Br (Gardner) - loaded at Port Talbot, left Solent, ETA Omaha 10th (Convoy EBC4W): returned to Southampton (Berth 108)

SAINT-ENOGAT 2,360/18 Br (MoWT) ex-French - left Humber 21st, via Thames, for Eastern Task Force area: returned 30th

SAINT RULE 524/41 Br (Gardner) - loaded at Port Talbot, left Bristol Channel 2nd, via Solent, for Omaha (intended for Convoy EBC3W ETA 9th): returned to Llanelly 11th

SAMBRE 349/30 Dutch - after loading, left Port Talbot 2nd, left Bristol Channel 5th, left Solent 9th for Omaha (Convoy EBC4W) but turned back: next recorded sailing - ETA Juno 1st July (Convoy ETC23W)

SAMUEL VERY 1,814/43 Br (MoWT) US - after loading, left Avonmouth 9th, left Bristol Channel 10th, ETA Utah 13th (Convoy EBC7)

SANDHILL 586/38 Br (Tyne-Tees) - left Thames 0215 5th, via Solent, for Eastern Task Force area (intended for Convoy ETC3W ETA 9th): returned 13th

SARD 410/09 Br (Kinnes) - loaded at London, left Thames 0215 5th, left Solent 2100 7th, ETA Juno 8th (Convoy ETC22W)

SARNIA 711/23 Br (Dorey) - loaded at Swansea, left Bristol Channel 30th May, via Solent (Anchorage 3N/b8) (intended for Assault Force O ETA Omaha 6th): returned to Fowey where arrived 2230 12th

SCHELDT 497/38 Br (Vianda) - loaded at Port Talbot, left Solent, ETA Omaha 13th (Convoy EBC7W): returned to Sharpness where arrived 20th

SEAVILLE 716/18 Br (Monks) - loaded at London, left Thames 0215 5th, via Solent, for Eastern Task Force area (intended for Convoy ETC3W ETA 9th): returned to Newhaven

SEDULITY 490/36 Br (Everard) - after loading, left London (King George V Dock) 19th May, left Thames 31st May, left Solent (Anchorage 3N/e8), arrived Juno 6th (Follow-up Convoy L1): discharged cargo of cased petrol and Bailey bridging 2100 6th-0100 8th: returned to London (Purfleet A)

SERENITY 557/41 Br (Everard) - ex Thames, left Solent, arrived Juno 12th (Convoy ETC6W): discharged cargo of cased petrol 1135 12th-2045 13th

SHERWOOD 1,530/24 Br (France, Fenwick) - ex London for Eastern Task Force area (intended for Convoy ETC2Z ETA 7th): returned 9th

SHERWOOD beached at Juno. [IWM A24012]

SIAK 1,150/30 Norwegian - left Bristol Channel, ETA Utah 10th (Convoy EBC4): returned to Penarth where arrived 18th

SIGNALITY 487/37 Br (Everard) - after loading, left London (King George V Dock) 19th May, left Thames 31st May, left Solent (Anchorage 3N/e9), arrived Juno 6th (Follow-up Convoy L1): discharged cargo of cased petrol and stores 2100 6th-1500 7th: returned to London (Purfleet B)

SIR EVELYN WOOD 850/96 Br (War Dept) - ex Thames, left Solent, ETA Juno 16th (Convoy ETC10W)

SKARV 852/23 Norwegian - loaded at Swansea, left Bristol Channel 30th May, via Solent (Anchorage 3N/b2) (intended for Assault Force O ETA Omaha 6th): returned to Fowey where arrived 2230 12th

SKELWITH FORCE 592/08 Br (Spratt) - after loading, left London (Tilbury) 16th May, left Thames 31st May, left Solent (Anchorage 3N/c8), arrived Juno 6th (Follow-up Convoy L1): discharged cargo of ammunition 2100 6th-1900 7th

SKUM 1,304/16 Norwegian - loaded at Newport, left Bristol Channel, ETA Omaha 10th (Convoy EBC4): returned to Penarth

SLEMISH 1,536/09 Br (Shamrock) - ex London for Eastern Task Force area (intended for Convoy ETC2Y ETA 7th): returned to London 10th

SOBORG 1,993/24 Br (MoWT) ex-Danish - (outward convoy unclear) returned from beach-head to Solent 9th

SODALITY 829/38 Br (Everard) - left Thames 0215 5th, via Solent, for Eastern Task Force area (intended for Convoy ETC3W ETA 9th): returned to Thames 13th/14th

SOJOURNER 435/20 Br (Taylor) - left for Eastern Task Force area 13th (Convoy ETC8) but, as loaded for Omaha, recalled: left Poole 24th, ETA Omaha 25th (EBC20W)

SOLLUND 941/08 Norwegian - after loading, left London 7th, left Solent, ETA Sword 13th (Convoy ETC7W)

SOUTHPORT 572/14 Br (Grace) - after loading, left London 30th May, left Thames 31st May, left Solent (Anchorage 4/c1), arrived Juno 0830 7th (Convoy EWC1B)

SPES 1,142/18 Norwegian - loaded at London, left Thames 0215 5th, left Solent 2100 7th, ETA Gold 8th (Convoy ETC22W)

SPHENE 815/20 Br (Robertson) - after loading, left Cardiff 10th, left Bristol Channel 11th, ETA Utah 14th (Convoy EBC8)

SPIRALITY 554/39 Br (Everard) - loaded at London, left Thames 0215 5th, left Solent 2100 7th, ETA Juno 8th (Convoy ETC22W)

STADION II 629/14 Norwegian - after loading, left London 3rd, left Thames 4th, left Solent, arrived Juno 0830 7th (Convoy EWC1B): returned to Southampton

STALEY BRIDGE 297/40 Br (Summers) - ex Port Talbot for Western Task Force area (intended for Convoy EBC2Y ETA 8th): returned to Southampton

STANLEY FORCE 586/20 Br (West Coast) - after loading, left London 30th May, left Thames 31st May, left Solent (Anchorage 3N/c6), arrived Gold 6th (Follow-up Convoy L1)

STANVILLE 538/18 Br (Monks) - loaded at Southampton, left Solent, ETA Utah 17th (Convoy EBC12W)

STARKENBORGH 878/41 Dutch - loaded at Sharpness, left Bristol Channel 30th May, via Solent (Anchorage 3N/d10) (intended for Assault Force U ETA Utah 6th): returned to Southampton 11th

STUART QUEEN 1,224/41 Br (British Channel Islands) - after loading, left Barry 3rd, left Solent, ETA Utah 7th (Convoy EWC1A): returned to Fowey where arrived 16th to load ammunition

SUMMITY   554/39   Br (Everard) - ex Thames, left Solent, ETA Sword 11th (Convoy ETC5W)

TEESWOOD   864/15   Br (Donking) - loaded at London, left Thames 31st May, left Solent (Anchorage 3S/a1), arrived Gold 0830 7th (Convoy EWC1B): returned to London where arrived 14th

THE BARON   820/27   Br (Hay) - after loading, left Cardiff 10th, left Bristol Channel 11th, ETA Utah 14th (Convoy EBC8)

THE EARL   926/36   Br (Hay) - loaded at Penarth, left Solent 11th, ETA Utah 12th (Convoy EBC6W)

THE PRESIDENT   926/36   Br (Hay) - loaded at Swansea, left Bristol Channel 30th May, via Solent (Anchorage 3N/b7) (intended for Assault Force O ETA Omaha 6th): returned to Fowey where arrived 2230 12th: on a subsequent voyage, badly holed in the storm and beached at Utah approx 21st, unable to return to UK under own steam

THE VICEROY   824/29   Br (Hay) - left Thames 0100 7th, left Solent, ETA Sword 10th (Convoy ETC4W): damaged by mine at Juno 13th

THESEUS   1,306/20   Dutch - after loading, left Newport 1st, left Bristol Channel 7th, ETA Omaha 10th (Convoy EBC4)

THORE HAFTE   626/96   Norwegian - ex Swansea for Western Task Force area (intended for Convoy EBC2Y ETA 8th): returned to Swansea 14th for repairs, instead of Fowey as planned

THORN   347/34   Br (Newry & Kilkeel) - withdrawn end May

THORNABY   1,174/35   Br (Tyne-Tees) - ex London for Eastern Task Force area (intended for Convoy ETC2Z ETA 7th): returned to London where arrived 16th

THYRA III   828/12   Br (MoWT) ex-Danish - ex London for Eastern Task Force area (intended for Convoy ETC2Z ETA 7th): returned to London (Berth 18, Tilbury Dock) where arrived 10th

TOMSK   1,229/11   Br (MoWT) ex-Danish - loaded at Swansea, left Bristol Channel 5th, ETA Utah 8th (Convoy EBC2Z): returned to Newport where arrived 18th

TOMSK beached. [IWM MH9092]

TON S.   466/37   Dutch - left Solent, ETA Juno 17th (Convoy ETC11W)

TOPAZ   577/20   Br (Robertson) - loaded at Penarth, left Bristol Channel 2nd, left Solent 1900 7th, ETA Utah 8th (Convoy EBC2W): returned to Southampton

TORFINN JARL   1,481/22   Norwegian - after loading, left Port Talbot 8th, left Bristol Channel 9th, ETA Omaha 12th (Convoy EBC6)

TORQUAY   870/14   Br (Davidson) - loaded at London, left Thames 31st May, left Solent (Anchorage 4/d9), arrived Juno 0830 7th (Convoy EWC1B)

TRES   946/17   Norwegian - left Thames 0215 5th, via Solent, for Eastern Task Force area (intended for Convoy ETC3W ETA 9th)

TROMP   391/32   Dutch - after loading, left London 25th May, left Solent, ETA Juno 11th (Convoy ETC5W)

TUDOR QUEEN   1,029/41   Br (British Channel Islands) - loaded at London, left Solent, ETA Sword 12th (Convoy ETC6W)

TULLY CROSBY   1,791/43   Br (MoWT) US - left Thames, ETA Gold 11th (Convoy ETC5): returned to London where arrived 17th: on a subsequent voyage, damaged by mine 30th but just able to return under own steam for repairs

ULSTER HERO   483/24   Br (Gardner) - loaded at Avonmouth, left Solent, ETA Utah 13th (Convoy EBC7W): returned to Southampton

VALBORG   844/14   Br (MoWT) ex-Danish - loaded at Penarth, left Bristol Channel 30th May (intended for Assault Force U ETA Utah 6th) but towed into Plymouth for steering gear repairs 1st: left Plymouth 1500 15th: after re-loading, left Fowey (via Dartmouth for shelter), ETA Western Task Force area 25th (Convoy EBC20) to discharge 856 dwt tons of ammunition: returned to London

VAN BRAKEL   398/29   Dutch - after loading, left Sharpness 1st, left Bristol Channel 2nd, via Solent, for Utah (intended for Convoy EBC3W ETA 9th)

VAREGG   943/10   Norwegian - ex Bristol Channel, left Solent, ETA Omaha 17th (Convoy EBC12W)

VESTMANROD   691/19   Norwegian - after loading, left London 30th May, left Thames 31st May, left Solent (Anchorage 3S/a6), arrived Juno 0830 7th (Convoy EWC1B): returned to Southampton where started loading 0930 18th

VESTMANROD beached in the Western Task Force area. [IWM KY30226]

WALDO HILL discharging off the beach-head. [IWM A24363]

VILK   1,944/13   Br (MoWT) ex-Estonian - ex London for Eastern Task Force area (intended for Convoy ETC2Y ETA 7th): returned 9th

VLIESTROOM   655/12   Dutch - loaded at Swansea, left Bristol Channel 2nd, left Solent 1900 7th, ETA Omaha 8th (Convoy EBC2W)

VULCANUS   1,819/07   Dutch - after loading, left Barry 9th, left Bristol Channel 12th, ETA Omaha 15th (Convoy EBC9): returned to Barry

WALDO HILL   1,791/43   Br (MoWT) US - arrived London 19th to load, left Thames, ETA Gold 26th (Convoy ETC18)

WALENBURGH   496/38   Dutch - ex Garston (did not sail as planned in Convoy EBC5W ETA 11th), left Sharpness 16th, ETA Omaha 19th (Convoy EBC14): returned to Sharpness

WALLACE ROSE   632/31   Br (Hughes) - after loading, left Penarth 30th May, arrived Solent (Anchorage 4/d6) 1st, left, arrived Utah 0600 7th (Convoy EWC1A): returned to Southampton: on a subsequent voyage, lost both anchors in storm 19th but ship kept under way off beach-head until 21st, ready to discharge cargo as soon as gales abated

WATERGATE 499/12   Br (Coppack) - after loading, left Plymouth 0529 12th, ETA Utah 13th (Convoy ECM5): returned to Plymouth

WATSON FERRIS 1,791/43   Br (MoWT) US - left Thames, ETA Gold 14th (Convoy ETC8)

WESTBURN 2,842/29   Br (Westwick) - loaded at Swansea, left Bristol Channel 5th, arrived Omaha 8th (Convoy EBC2Z): returned to Barry

WESTDALE 424/11   Br (Ohlson) - loaded at Avonmouth, left Bristol Channel 2nd, left Solent 1900 7th, ETA Utah 8th (Convoy EBC2W): on a subsequent voyage, arrived Gold 1000 18th to discharge 215 tons ammunition and carbide: 0200 20th mine exploded while vessel was steaming slowly to her anchors in gale: ship allowed to drift to beach but grounded ¼ mile from shore and sank at 0930, cargo of ammunition being salved. *[Later salved and hulked]*

WESTLAND 426/31   Dutch - loaded at London, left Thames 31st May, left Solent (Anchorage 3N/d12), arrived Sword 6th (Follow-up Convoy L1)

WESTON 485/20   Br (ICI) - after loading, left London 2nd, left Thames 0215 5th, left Solent 2100 7th, ETA Sword 8th (Convoy ETC22W)

WESTOWN 710/21   Br (Grace) - left Thames, ETA Sword 10th (Convoy ETC4): returned to Poole: on a subsequent voyage, storm damaged and beached at Utah approx 21st

WHEATCROP 523/24   Br (Spillers) - after loading, left Penarth 1st, left Bristol Channel 2nd, left Solent 1900 7th, ETA Utah 8th (Convoy EBC2W): returned to Southampton: under repair 20th

WILD ROSE 873/21   Br (Hughes) - loaded at Swansea, left Bristol Channel 5th for Western Task Force area (intended for Convoy EBC2Y ETA 8th): returned to Southampton

WILLIAM BURSLEY 1,791/43   Br (MoWT) US - after loading, left Barry 10th, ETA Omaha 13th (Convoy EBC7): returned to Swansea

WILLIAM H. DANIELS 1,772/23   Canadian - ex London for Eastern Task Force area (intended for Convoy ETC2Y ETA 7th): was at beach-head discharging mixed cargo 1900 15th-1900 18th

WILLIAM HOMAN 1,793/43   Br (MoWT) US - after loading, left London 12th, left Thames, ETA Gold 15th (Convoy ETC9)

WILLIAM HOWLAND 1,792/43   Br (MoWT) US - ex Thames for Eastern Task Force area (intended for Convoy ETC3 ETA 9th): returned to Thames where arrived 16th

WILNO 2,018/26   Polish - left Thames 0100 7th, via Solent, for Eastern Task Force area: returned to Cardiff where arrived 17th

WINONA 2,174/06   Canadian - ex London for Eastern Task Force area (intended for Convoy ETC2Z ETA 7th): returned to Thames where arrived 10th

WINONA off the French coast shortly after D-Day. [IWM A24036]

Coasters arriving off Juno on 7th June, 1944. [IWM B5208]

WOOLER   507/36   Br (Tyne-Tees) - ex Garston for Western Task Force area (intended for Convoy EBC2Y ETA 8th): returned to Port Talbot

YEWGLEN   607/15   Br (Stewart) - after loading, left London 30th May, left Thames 31st May, left Solent (Anchorage 3S/a2), arrived Gold 0830 7th (Convoy EWC1B): on a subsequent voyage, damaged and beached at Sword 23rd

YEWMOUNT   859/39   Br (Stewart) - ex Thames, left Solent, ETA Gold 12th (Convoy ETC6W): returned to Sharpness

YEWPARK   827/30   Br (Stewart) - loaded at London, left Thames 31st May, left Solent (Anchorage 3S/a5), arrived Gold 0830 7th (Convoy EWC1B)

YEWTREE   826/28   Br (Stewart) - ex Thames, left Solent, ETA Gold 13th (Convoy ETC7W)

YOKEFLEET   844/10   Br (Ouse) - after loading, left London 17th, left Thames, ETA Juno 19th (Convoy ETC13)

ZEELAND   2,726/30   Dutch - loaded at Swansea, left Bristol Channel 5th, ETA Omaha 8th (Convoy EBC2Z): returned to Barry

ZEELAND   421/30   Dutch - after loading, left London 25th May, left Thames, left Solent, ETA Gold 13th (Convoy ETC7W)

ZELO   2,294/21   Br (Pelton) - after loading, left London 9th, left Thames, ETA Gold 12th (Convoy ETC6)

ZUIDERHAVEN   315/41   Dutch - left Thames 0100 7th, left Solent, ETA Juno 10th (Convoy ETC4W)

ZUIDLAND   426/31   Dutch - ex Thames, left Solent, ETA Juno 12th (Convoy ETC6W)

ZUIJDERBURGH   2,630/06   Dutch - after loading, left Barry 11th, left Bristol Channel 13th, ETA Utah 16th (Convoy EBC10)

Section A4 - TANK LANDING SHIPS
AND
ASSAULT LANDING CRAFT

The Force L tank landing ship, LST 319, arrives in the Eastern Task Force area. [IWM]

(All dates are June 1944 unless otherwise stated.)

LANDING SHIPS, TANK (LST)

Named LSTs. Tonnage/year of build, nationality (owner) - origin and assembly area, destination and convoy of first sailing: other information.

BACHAQUERO 4,890/37 Br (Lago) tanker as HM LST(1) (capacity 18 tanks or 33 trucks: 207 troops) - loaded at London (Tilbury Dock), left Thames for Eastern Task Force area (Follow-up Convoy L3): became Rhino depot ship at Sword 8th: damaged by gunfire 14th and by mine 23rd: returned 28th

MISOA 4,800/37 Br (Lago) tanker as HM LST(1) (capacity 18 tanks or 33 trucks: 192 troops) - loaded at London (Tilbury Dock), left Thames for Eastern Task Force area (Follow-up Convoy L3): became Rhino depot ship at Gold: left for Thames 1st July

TASAJERA 4,308/38 Br (Lago) tanker as HM LST(1) (capacity 18 tanks or 33 trucks: 207 troops) - loaded at London (Tilbury Dock), left Thames for Eastern Task Force area (Follow-up Convoy L3): became Rhino depot ship at Juno 8th: holed in collision with Gooseberry 4 and grounded after dragging anchor in gale 19th

LST 322 on 8th June, 1944, with two towed barges astern. [IWM]

Unnamed LSTs (Typical capacity 8 jeeps, 21x3-ton and 6x15-cwt trucks and 18 tanks: 177 troops). The following were allocated to Operation Neptune: those marked * HM LST(2), others US -

FORCE U - loaded at Dartmouth, Brixham and Plymouth, left Dartmouth, Tor Bay and Salcombe 5th, arrived Utah 6th (Assault Convoys U2B, U3 and U4)

LST 46, 47, 48, 49, 50, 57, 58, 230, 281, 282, 283, 284, 290, 294, 311, 346, 351, 371, 380, 382, 400, 491, 492, 499, 500, 501, 508, 509, 515, 539

FORCE O - loaded at Portland Harbour, left Portland Harbour 5th, arrived Omaha 6th

LST 6, 51, 75, 133, 134, 157, 285, 286, 309, 310, 314, 315, 316, 317, 332, 347, 350, 357, 372, 373, 374, 375, 376, 502

FORCE G - loaded in Solent area, left Solent (Anchorages 4 and 5) 1618-1926 5th, arrived Gold 1210-1500 6th (Assault Convoys G11C, G13D, G17A and G18A)

LST 1, 2, 17, 21, 25, 30, 44, 52, 72, 73, 229, 264, 279, 280, 287, 293, 308, 312, 344, 345, 359, 370, 377, 378, 379, 493, 503, 519, 520

FORCE J - loaded in Solent area, left Solent (Anchorages 18, 20W and 22) 1900-2145 5th, arrived Juno 6th (Assault Convoys J15 and J16)

LST 8*, 11*, 62*, 65*, 80*, 159*, 160*, 180*, 199*, 215*, 238*, 239*, 323*, 368*, 402*, 404*, 405*, 409*, 410*, 413*, 416*, 421*, 425*

FORCE S - loaded in Solent area, left Solent (Anchorages 23N and 26N) 5th, arrived Sword 6th (Assault Convoys S13, S14A, S14B and S15)

LST 302*, 303*, 304*, 320*, 322*, 324*, 361*, 363*, 364*, 365*, 367*, 408*, 412*, 419*, 420*, 423*, 427*, 428*

FORCE B - loaded at Falmouth and Plymouth, left Fowey, Helford River, Falmouth and Plymouth, arrived Western Task Force area 6th/7th (Follow-up Convoys B1 and B3/ECL1)

LST 5, 7, 16, 27, 28, 53, 54, 55, 56, 59, 61, 212, 262, 266, 288, 289, 291, 292, 306, 307, 325, 331, 335, 336, 337, 338, 355, 356, 369, 388, 389, 391, 392, 393, 494, 495, 496, 497, 498, 504, 505, 506, 510, 511, 512, 516, 523, 532, 533, 538

FORCE L - loaded at Felixstowe, left Harwich and Thames, arrived Eastern Task Force area 6th (Follow-up Convoy L1)

LST 63*, 137, 165*, 175, 176, 198*, 200*, 208, 209, 214*, 237*, 261, 301*, 319*, 321*, 366*, 403*, 406*, 530, 534, 540

- loaded at London (Tilbury Dock), left Thames, arrived Eastern Task Force area 6th (Follow-up Convoy L3)

LST 60, 138, 139, 295, 327, 360, 383, 384, 385, 386, 517, 521, 522, 524, 527, 528, 529, 535, 536, 537, 541, 542, 543, 682, 980, 981, 982, 983

- loaded in Solent area, left Solent (Anchorage 26N), arrived Sword 7th (Follow-up Convoy L5/ETM1)

LST 162*, 163*, 164*, 415*, 430*

Other LSTs

LST 9*, 161* (delayed at Plymouth for repairs), 197, 326, 381, 401* (delayed at Newcastle for repairs)

LSTs lost during June

LST 314, 376, 496, 499, 523

ASSAULT LANDING CRAFT
The following were assigned -
Landing Craft, Infantry (Small)
Assembled Solent area

LCI(S) 501-510, 512-540

Landing Craft, Infantry (Large)
Assembled Dartmouth, the Medway, Newhaven, Portsmouth, Plymouth, Southampton and Weymouth

LCI(L) 3-5, 8-16, 33, 35, 75, 83-96, 103-106, 109-111, 115-118, 121-123, 125-127, 129-131, 134-136, 164-166, 169, 171, 172, 174-183, 193, 209-219, 229, 231, 232, 238, 241-244, 246, 249, 250, 252, 255, 256, 262, 263, 266, 268, 270, 271, 276, 277, 285, 288, 291, 295, 298-302, 305-307, 310, 311, 313, 319-326, 349, 350, 374-391, 400, 401, 403, 408-421, 487-502, 505-517, 520-530, 537-542, 551-557

Landing Craft, Personnel (Large)
Assembled Solent area

LCP(L) 3, 4, 7, 13, 19, 20-23, 28, 31, 34, 37, 40, 41, 43, 44, 46, 47, 51, 53, 84-86, 88, 94, 95, 97, 98, 102, 110, 114, 115, 118-122, 124, 125, 127-135, 137, 143-153, 155, 156, 158, 160-163, 165-168, 170-173, 175, 176, 178, 179, 186-189, 191, 192, 195-200, 202, 207, 208, 211, 229-248, 265, 266, 268-270, 272-275, 278-280, 282-286, 288, 293-296, 298-313

US Landing Craft, Tank (Marks 4, 5 and 6)

Assembled Dartmouth, Falmouth and Portland

LCT(4)/(5)/(6) 3, 7, 18, 20, 22, 25, 27, 29, 30, 80, 147-149, 153, 195, 197, 199-202, 205-207, 209-211, 213, 214, 217-219, 221, 244, 271, 276, 290, 293, 294, 305, 332, 362, 364, 413, 415, 431, 434, 443, 447, 456-460, 474-476, 486, 489, 492, 495, 497, 510, 511, 515-520, 522, 524-553, 555, 564, 569-573, 580, 581, 583-603, 607-609, 611-626, 637-654, 657-659, 662-667, 703-715, 763-769, 775-780, 809-815, 833, 851-856

LCT 1046 at Mulberry A on 13th June, 1944.

HM Landing Craft, Tank (Marks 3, 4, 5 and 6)

Assembled Brixham, Dartmouth, Harwich, Newhaven, Plymouth, Portland, Shoreham, Solent and Southampton

LCT(3)/(4)/(5)/(6) 302, 303, 306, 311, 313, 317, 318, 320, 324, 341, 345, 354, 372, 382, 384, 390, 399, 411, 413, 422, 427-433, 441-444, 451, 453-456, 461-463, 465-472, 474-476, 500-504, 506-526, 528-534, 539, 541, 543-546, 555, 558, 562, 564-566, 568, 569, 571, 573-577, 593, 597-600, 602, 604, 608-612, 627-632, 634-641, 643-647, 649-652, 656, 664-679, 683-685, 689-692, 700, 703, 704, 706-713, 715-721, 723, 724, 726-733, 735, 737, 739, 748-753, 755-763, 765-770, 781-790, 793-805, 807-810, 813-815, 821, 822, 824, 826-829, 832, 833, 836-838, 851-861, 863, 864, 875, 876, 878, 879, 881-887, 889, 891, 892, 894, 896-905, 907, 909, 920-938, 940-947, 950-954, 956-961, 964-970, 974, 975, 977-981, 996-1003, 1006, 1008-1011, 1013-1020, 1022-1028, 1030-1035, 1037-1043, 1045-1051, 1065-1074, 1076-1088, 1092-1099, 1106, 1118-1127, 1162-1164, 1166, 1168-1171, 1315, 2002, 2004, 2011, 2013, 2038, 2040, 2041, 2044-2047, 2049-2051, 2053, 2055-2057, 2073-2079, 2130, 2131, 2135, 2138, 2150, 2186, 2188, 2189, 2193, 2194, 2226, 2229, 2230, 2232, 2234, 2235, 2240, 2243, 2246, 2261, 2269, 2270, 2272, 2285-2287, 2289, 2292, 2295-2297, 2302-2304, 2306, 2307, 2313, 2331, 2336-2339, 2343, 2363, 2399, 2421, 2423-2425, 2427, 2429, 2436, 2437, 2439-2441, 2477, 2479, 2483-2485, 2487, 2498, 2627, 2628, 7006-7013, 7034-7036, 7039, 7043-7054, 7057, 7058, 7063-7092, 7096-7102

Landing Craft, Vehicle (Personnel)

Assembled Beaulieu River, Hayling Island and Portsmouth area

LCV(P) 1005-1017, 1022-1039, 1041-1060, 1062-1065, 1067, 1074-1211, 1215-1228, 1230, 1235-1257, 1259-1266

Other craft were embarked in ships

PART B

THE MAIN NAVAL SUPPORT SHIPS AND CRAFT

Section B1 - ASSAULT HEADQUARTERS SHIPS AND CRAFT

ANCON [IWM]

These were vessels of a variety of types, including cruisers, a gunboat, frigates, destroyers, converted passenger vessels, a yacht and landing craft, specifically allocated to the initial assault fleet to serve as flagships, LSH (Landing Ship, Headquarters) and control vessels.

NAME OF VESSEL   Tonnage/year of build, nationality (owner) of merchant ships, type - origin and/or assembly area, destination and convoy of first sailing: other information. (All dates are June 1944 unless otherwise stated.)

ALBRIGHTON   HM destroyer (Hunt class) as LSH Force G3 - left Solent (Anchorage 5/a12) 5th, arrived Gold 6th (Assault Convoy G16B): became Ferry Craft HQ ship 8th

ANCON   10,021/39   US vessel as HQ ship Force O - left Plymouth, via Portland Harbour anchorage, arrived Omaha 0251 6th (Assault Convoy O1)

AUGUSTA   US cruiser as Flagship Naval Commander, Western Task Force, and bombarding force reserve ship - left Plymouth Sound anchorage 5th, arrived Omaha 6th (Assault Convoy O1)

BAYFIELD   7,985/43   US attack transport (APA) (capacity 1,545 troops) as HQ ship Force U - embarkation at Plymouth, left Plymouth Sound anchorage 0943 5th, arrived Utah 0229 6th (Assault Convoy U1A): returned 25th

LARGS [IWM]

BULOLO 6,267/38 Australian (Burns, Philp) liner as HM LSH Force G - after embarkation, left Southampton (Berth 41) 1710 3rd, left Solent (Anchorage 5/a1) 1837 5th, arrived Gold 0556 6th (Assault Convoy G9A): damaged by bomb near operations room 0605 7th: upperworks superficially damaged when rammed by EMPIRE PITT 15th: hit by LCT 1010 27th: 1425 27th left for Southampton (Berth 20) where arrived 1212 28th

DACRES HM US frigate as LSH Force S2 - switched with GOATHLAND end May: left Portsmouth Harbour 5th, after embarkation off Newhaven, left 1215 5th, arrived Sword 6th (Assault Convoy S10): assisted the salvage of JAMES A. FARRELL 29th

GOATHLAND HM destroyer (Hunt class) as LSH Force S3 - switched with DACRES end May: after embarkation at quay, left Portsmouth Harbour 1320 5th, arrived Sword 6th (Assault Convoy S5)

HILARY 7,403/31 Br (Booth) liner as HM LSH Force J (carried 6 landing craft) - embarkation at Southampton by tender, left Solent (Anchorage 19W/2), left Spithead Gate 1925 5th, arrived Juno 0558 6th (Assault Convoy J11): suffered slight damage in bomb near miss 0410 13th: became Flagship, Eastern Task Force, 24th

KINGSMILL HM US frigate as LSH Force G2 - embarkation at Southampton (New Docks), left Solent (Anchorage 5/a7), arrived Gold 6th (Assault Convoy G10A): ferry control HQ ship 19th-23rd and 24th-30th

LARGS 4,504/38 French passenger vessel CHARLES PLUMIER as HM LSH Force S - ex Portsmouth Harbour jetty, left Solent (Anchorage 25/5) 2145 5th, arrived Sword 6th (Assault Convoy S7): slightly damaged by mine 0045 25th and by gunfire 1830 28th: returned to Solent 30th when Sword beach-head closed

LAWFORD HM US frigate as LSH Force J1 - embarkation at Southampton (Berth 38), left Solent (Anchorage 19W) 5th, arrived Juno 6th (Assault Convoy J9): 0503 8th broke in two as a result of an air attack, bow and stern sections remaining visible above the water

LOCUST   HM gunboat as LSH Force S1 - left Portsmouth Harbour jetty, left Spithead Gate 1935 5th, arrived Sword 6th (Assault Convoy S12): damaged by gunfire at Sword approx 16th

LOTHIAN   8,036/38   Br (Ellerman) liner CITY OF EDINBURGH as HM reserve LSH - left Forth 6th, arrived Harwich 8th

NITH   HM frigate as LSH Force G1 - embarkation at Southampton (New Docks), left Solent (Anchorage 5/a2) 5th, arrived Gold 6th (Assault Convoy G9C): damaged by bomb at Gold 2321 24th

ROYAL ULSTERMAN   3,244/36   Br (Burns & Laird) cross-Channel passenger vessel as HM LSI(H) acting as LSH Force J3 and reserve LSH Force J (carried 6 landing craft) - embarkation at Southampton (Berth 37), left Solent (Anchorage 19E/1) 1600 5th, arrived Juno 0808 6th (Assault Convoy J14): became HQ ship for Captain north and southbound convoys 26th

ST ADRIAN   387/27   Yacht as HM special service vessel serving as ferry control HQ ship Force S - left Portsmouth Harbour jetty 5th, arrived Sword 6th (Assault Convoy S5): rescued survivors from SVENNER 6th

SCYLLA   HM cruiser as Flagship Naval Commander, Eastern Task Force - left Portsmouth Harbour buoys 1340 5th, left Solent (Anchorage 26N) 1627 5th, arrived Sword 0415 6th: damaged by mine 2256 23rd, while moving from Juno to Sword: towed by tugs ENVOY and THAMES to Solent where arrived 1726 24th then 25th/26th towed to Sheerness by tug BLACK ROCK. *[Not repaired]*

WAVENEY   HM frigate as LSH Force J2 - embarkation at Southampton (Berth 39), left Solent (Anchorage 19E/2) 5th, arrived Juno 6th (Assault Convoy J10): ferry control HQ ship 23rd

Assigned craft

LCC (Landing Craft, Control) **10**, **20**, **30**, **40**, **50**, **60**, **70**, **80**, **90**

LCH (Landing Craft, Headquarters) **98**, **100**, **167**, **168**, **185**, **187**, **239**, **245**, **269**, **275**, **317**

SCYLLA in action on D-Day, in the distance a 'Glen' (left) and an 'Empire' infantry landing ship.
[IWM A24100]

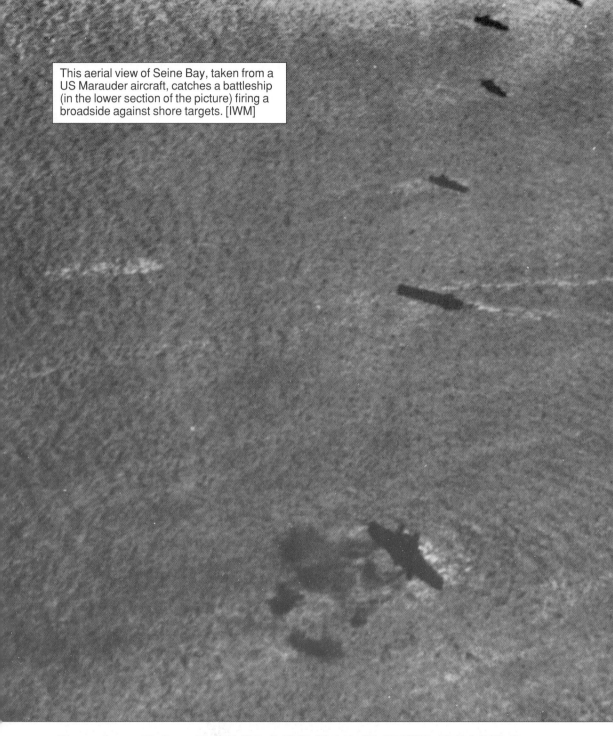

This aerial view of Seine Bay, taken from a US Marauder aircraft, catches a battleship (in the lower section of the picture) firing a broadside against shore targets. [IWM]

Section B2 - BOMBARDING BATTLESHIPS, MONITORS, CRUISERS AND DUTCH GUNBOATS

Divided into Forces A, C, K, E and F, with pre-arranged targets in the Utah, Omaha, Gold, Juno and Sword sectors respectively, the faster units of the bombarding fleet set sail from Belfast or the Clyde on the 2nd and 3rd. Off the English south coast, they were joined by the slower units, all to reach the Normandy beach-head early on the morning of D-Day. After using their firepower in support of the landings, most returned to English ports, as required, to re-ammunition before resuming bombardment duties off the beach-head and some, on the 25th, off Cherbourg.

NAME OF VESSEL   Nationality, (main armament) type - origin and/or assembly area and details of first sailing: other information. (All dates are June 1944 unless otherwise stated.)

AJAX   HM (6" gun) cruiser - left Clyde 1100 3rd, arrived Eastern Task Force area 0528 6th and opened fire against shore targets 0530 (Bombarding Force K) (Assault Convoy G12)

ARETHUSA   HM (6" gun) cruiser - left Clyde 1913 2nd, arrived Eastern Task Force area 0455 6th (Bombarding Force D) (Assault Convoy S6): expended 392 rounds of main ammunition by 1600 6th: returned to Portsmouth 14th: left Portsmouth Harbour jetty 0808 16th carrying HM The King on a day visit to beach-head, arrived Juno 1240, left 1700, arrived Portsmouth 2050: internally damaged by mine 25th

ARGONAUT   HM (5.25" gun) cruiser - left Clyde 1130 3rd, anchored Eastern Task Force area 0630 6th and provided notable gunfire support that day (Bombarding Force K) (Assault Convoy G12): returned to Solent where arrived 2126 12th

ARKANSAS   US (12" gun) battleship - left Belfast Lough 0200 3rd, arrived Western Task Force area and opened fire against shore targets 0538 6th (Bombarding Force C) (Assault Convoy O1)

BELFAST   HM (6" gun) cruiser - left Clyde 1055 3rd, arrived Eastern Task Force area 0500 6th (Bombarding Force E) (Assault Convoy G14): returned to Solent where arrived 0004 11th. *[Vessel now preserved in London]*

BELLONA   HM (5.25" gun) cruiser - left Belfast Lough 0752 3rd, left Plymouth 1450 5th, arrived Western Task Force area 0617 6th (Bombarding Force reserve): shot down an attacking aircraft 0030 9th: returned to Plymouth where arrived 0805 16th

BLACK PRINCE   HM (5.25" gun) cruiser - left Belfast Lough 0800 3rd, arrived Western Task Force area 0502 6th and came under shore battery gunfire: provided notable gunfire support starting 0545 that day (Bombarding Force A) (Assault Convoy U1A): returned to Plymouth (F Buoy) where arrived 1710 16th

DANAE   HM (6" gun) cruiser - left Clyde 1859 2nd, arrived Eastern Task Force area 0507 6th (Bombarding Force D) (Assault Convoy S6): expended 50 rounds of main ammunition by 1600 6th: 1700 6th left for Solent where arrived 2253: left for beach-head to become depot ship (Gooseberry 5) 12th

DIADEM   HM (5.25" gun) cruiser - left Clyde 1100 3rd, arrived Eastern Task Force area 0500 6th and opened fire against shore targets at 0550 (Bombarding Force E) (Assault Convoy G14): returned to Solent, where arrived 2335 12th, then to beach-head 14th: ship's port side holed in five places by Rhino ferry alongside LLOYDCREST 19th

DRAGON   Polish (6" gun) cruiser - left Clyde 2nd, arrived Eastern Task Force area 6th (Bombarding Force D) (Assault Convoy S6): expended 50 rounds of main ammunition by 1600 6th. (See also note at end of Section C2)

EMERALD   HM (6" gun) cruiser - left Clyde 1050 3rd, arrived Eastern Task Force area 0450 6th (Bombarding Force K) (Assault Convoy G12): oil fuel tank ruptured by near miss 7th: returned to Solent 16th

ENTERPRISE   HM (6" gun) cruiser - left Belfast Lough 0754 3rd, arrived Western Task Force area 0350 6th (Bombarding Force A) (Assault Convoy U1A): returned to Solent where arrived 2034 11th

EREBUS   HM (15" gun) monitor - left Weymouth Bay (Anchorage H7) 1630 5th, arrived Western Task Force area 0420 6th and opened fire against shore targets 0635 (Bombarding Force A) (Assault

(Above) HM cruiser
BELFAST in
September 1944.
[IWM A25665]

(Right) The Dutch
gunboat FLORES at
anchor on D-Day.
[IWM MISC29609]

(Below) The US
cruiser QUINCY.
[IWM A 24307]

(Above) The battleship USS NEVADA. [IWM A24312] (Below) HM monitor EREBUS. [IWM]

Convoy U1A): 1643 6th, port gun barrel split open rendering turret unfit for further use: returned to Portland where arrived 0714 9th

FLORES   Dutch (5.9" gun) gunboat - left Solent (Anchorage 22/a10) 1730 5th, arrived Eastern Task Force area 0515 6th (Bombarding Force K) (Assault Convoy G12): returned to Solent 17th

FROBISHER   HM (7.5" gun) cruiser - left Clyde 1906 2nd, arrived Eastern Task Force area 0515 6th (Bombarding Force D) (Assault Convoy S6): expended 78 rounds of main ammunition by 1600 6th: returned to Solent where arrived 0137 9th having fired 494 rounds of main ammunition: became depot ship (Mulberry B) where arrived 1748 12th: landing barge collided with stern 0300 24th

GEORGES LEYGUES   French (6" gun) cruiser - left Belfast Lough 3rd, arrived Western Task Force area 6th (Bombarding Force C) (Assault Convoy O1)

GLASGOW   HM (6" gun) cruiser - left Belfast Lough 0230 3rd, arrived Western Task Force area 6th: opened fire 0554 and provided notable gunfire support that day (Bombarding Force C) (Assault Convoy O1): returned to Solent where arrived 1118 11th: damaged by gunfire (two hits, one near miss) during Cherbourg bombardment 25th

HAWKINS   HM (7.5" gun) cruiser - left Belfast Lough 0752 3rd, arrived Western Task Force area 0215 6th and opened fire 0538 (Bombarding Force A) (Assault Convoy U1A): returned to Solent where arrived 2355 10th: 1410 15th left Solent to became depot ship (Gooseberry 4)

MAURITIUS   HM (6" gun) cruiser - left Clyde 1905 2nd, arrived Eastern Task Force area 0515 6th, opened fire on three small craft 0530 6th (Bombarding Force D) (Assault Convoy S6): expended 260 rounds of main ammunition by 1600 6th: splinter damaged by bombs 0025 13th: returned to Solent where arrived 1830 15th

MONTCALM   French (6" gun) cruiser - left Belfast Lough 3rd, arrived Western Task Force area 6th (Bombarding Force C) (Assault Convoy O1)

NELSON   HM (16" gun) battleship - left Scapa 1510 2nd, via Milford Haven and Plymouth, left Solent 0557 11th, arrived Gold 1236 same day (Bombarding Force reserve): superficially damaged by mine 1930 18th en route to Solent where arrived 0005 19th en route for Philadelphia

NEVADA   US (14" gun) battleship - left Belfast Lough 0222 3rd, arrived Western Task Force area and opened fire against shore targets 0547 6th, providing notable gunfire support that day (Bombarding Force A) (Assault Convoy U1A): returned to Plymouth where arrived 0522 9th

ORION   HM (6" gun) cruiser - left Clyde 1100 3rd, arrived Eastern Task Force area and provided notable gunfire support 6th (Bombarding Force K) (Assault Convoy G12)

QUINCY   US (8" gun) cruiser - left Belfast Lough 3rd, arrived Western Task Force area and opened fire 0537 6th, providing notable gunfire support that day (Bombarding Force A) (Assault Convoy U1A)

RAMILLIES   HM (15" gun) battleship - left Clyde 1925 2nd, arrived Eastern Task Force area and opened fire against shore targets 0510 6th, providing notable gunfire support that day (Bombarding Force D) (Assault Convoy S6): expended 154 rounds of main ammunition by 1600 6th: returned to Solent where arrived 0717 7th

ROBERTS   HM (15" gun) monitor - (lack of speed precluded her from sailing from the Clyde with other units of the Force) left Solent (Anchorage 25/8) 1730 5th, arrived Eastern Task Force area 0520 6th (Bombarding Force D) (Assault Convoy S6): provided notable gunfire support: expended 69 rounds of main ammunition by 1600 6th: 2130 6th starboard gun became defective but vessel continued in action with port gun: returned to Solent (Anchorage 25/8) where arrived 1011 7th

RODNEY   HM (16" gun) battleship - left Clyde 1400 3rd, left Solent 0253 7th, ran down and sank LCT 427 at 0304 en route for Sword then Juno (Bombarding Force reserve)

SIRIUS   HM (5.25" gun) cruiser - left Clyde 3rd, left Solent 0300 7th for Eastern Task Force area (Bombarding Force reserve)

HM battleship RODNEY off Normandy. [IWM A23958]

SOEMBA   Dutch (5.9" gun) gunboat - left Plymouth anchorage 5th, arrived Western Task Force area 6th (Bombarding Force A) (Assault Convoy U2A2)

TEXAS   US (14" gun) battleship - left Belfast Lough 0215 3rd, arrived Western Task Force area, opened fire against shore targets 0550 6th and provided notable gunfire support that day (Bombarding Force C) (Assault Convoy O1): returned to Plymouth where arrived 2230 9th: damaged by gunfire during Cherbourg bombardment 25th

TUSCALOOSA   US (8" gun) cruiser - left Belfast Lough 3rd, arrived Western Task Force area and provided notable gunfire support 6th (Bombarding Force A) (Assault Convoy U1A)

WARSPITE   HM (15" gun) battleship - left Clyde 1926 2nd, arrived Eastern Task Force area 0525 6th and provided notable gunfire support that day (Bombarding Force D) (Assault Convoy S6): expended 219 rounds of main ammunition by 1600 6th: suffered superficial blast damage 7th: returned to Solent where arrived 0310 8th: damaged by mine explosion port side aft off Harwich 0747 13th, while en route from beach-head to Rosyth to change guns

HM battleship WARSPITE on D-Day. [IWM A23914]

A US destroyer makes smoke on 25th June, 1944. [IWM A24308]

Section B3 - DESTROYERS except those forming part of the
Anti-Submarine Screen (which listed in Section B5)

On the eve of D-Day, destroyers carried out patrols at the eastern and western ends of the English Channel to act as guardships against possible German surface vessel attack. Others headed towards the Normandy coast, accompanying the bombarding fleets from Belfast and the Clyde, and from West Country ports, the Solent and the Thames Estuary, escorting the assault vessels. Off the beach-head many of the destroyers performed invaluable service providing inshore gunfire support.

NAME OF VESSEL   Nationality - origin and/or assembly area, destination and details of first sailing: other information. (All dates are June 1944 unless otherwise stated.)

ALGONQUIN   Canadian - left Solent (Anchorage 31/f4) 1650 5th, arrived Juno 6th (Assault Convoy J11 escort) and provided gunfire support

ASHANTI   HM - ex Plymouth on patrol (Hurd Deep area) 5th/6th: one German destroyer [ZH1] sunk and another damaged in action off Ushant early a.m. 9th: in action against German minesweepers which were sunk or damaged SW of Jersey early a.m. 14th

AVON VALE   HM (Hunt class) - left Thames 5th for Eastern Task Force area (Follow-up Convoy L1 escort)

BALDWIN   US - left Weymouth Bay 5th, arrived Omaha 6th (Assault Convoy O1 escort) and provided gunfire support, suffering slight damage from enemy action that day: in action against E-boat 0040 9th

BARTON   US - left Plymouth 5th, arrived Utah 6th (Assault Convoy U2A2 escort) and allocated to Omaha for gunfire support: slightly damaged by gunfire during Cherbourg bombardment 25th

BEAGLE   HM - left Solent (Anchorage 22/e3) 1400 5th, arrived Juno 6th (Assault Convoy J8 escort): escorted convoy which lost LSTs 314 and 376 to E-boat attack 9th: opened fire on E-boat 0051 26th: towed PINK to Solent 27th

BLANKNEY   HM (Hunt class) - left Solent (Anchorage 4/a4) 5th, arrived Gold 6th (Assault Convoy G15 escort)

BLEASDALE   HM (Hunt class) - left Solent (Anchorage 4/a9) 5th, arrived Juno 6th (Assault Convoy J10 escort) and provided gunfire support

BLENCATHRA   HM (Hunt class) - left Bristol Channel 6th, arrived Western Task Force area 8th (Convoy EBP2 escort)

BLYSKAWICA   Polish - ex Plymouth on patrol: in action against German destroyers off Ushant early a.m. 9th: carried the C-in-C Polish Armed Forces on visit to beach-head 27th

BOADICEA   HM - left Falmouth 5th, arrived Western Task Force area 6th (Follow-up Convoy B3/U4/ECL1 escort): on a subsequent voyage, hit in forward magazine by aerial torpedo 0445 13th: fore part of ship disintegrated and after part sank rapidly

BRISSENDEN   HM (Hunt class) - left Plymouth anchorage 5th, arrived Western Task Force area 6th (Follow-up Convoy B1 escort): returned to Portland (OCEANWAY escort) 6th: in action against E-boats night 12th/13th

BULLDOG   HM - replaced mid May by HARGOOD

BULMER   US - escorted northbound convoy 18th

BUTLER   US - left Belfast Lough 3rd, arrived Utah 6th (Assault Convoy U1A escort)

CAMPBELL   HM - left Solent (Anchorage 26N/a11) 5th, arrived Sword 6th (Assault Convoy S13 escort)

CARMICK   US - left Weymouth Bay 1130 5th, arrived Omaha 6th (minesweeper escort) and provided gunfire support

CATTISTOCK   HM (Hunt class) - left Solent (Anchorage 3N/a10) 5th, arrived Gold 6th (Assault Convoy G1 minesweeper escort): gunfire support vessel

CORRY   US - left Plymouth 5th, on arrival Utah 6th (Assault Convoy U2B escort) hit mine approx 0645 and sank

COTSWOLD   HM (Hunt class) - left Thames 5th for Eastern Task Force area (Follow-up Convoy L1 escort)

COTTESMORE   HM (Hunt class) - left Solent (Anchorage 4/a3) 5th, arrived Gold 6th (Assault Convoy G2 minesweeper escort): gunfire support vessel

DAVIS   US - arrived Clyde 2200 1st en route to beach-head (convoy escort): heavily damaged by mine 21st

CATTISTOCK off the beach-head with tank landing ships in the distance. [IWM A23909]

FURY went aground on 22nd June, 1944. [IWM B6068]

DOYLE   US - left Weymouth Bay 5th, arrived Omaha 6th (Assault Convoy O1 minesweeper escort) and provided gunfire support

DUNCAN   HM - left Milford Haven 6th (HMS NELSON escort)

EGLINTON   HM (Hunt class) - left Solent (Anchorage 26N/a4), left Spithead Gate 2130 5th, arrived Sword 6th (Assault Convoy S7 escort): gunfire support vessel: rescued survivors from MAID OF ORLEANS 28th

ELLYSON   US - left Plymouth 5th, arrived Western Task Force area 6th (Follow-up Convoy B2 escort)

EMMONS   US - replaced ENDICOTT: left Weymouth Bay 5th, arrived Omaha 6th (Assault Convoy O1 minesweeper escort) and provided gunfire support

ENDICOTT   US - withdrawn end May for collision damage repairs

ESKIMO   HM - ex Plymouth on patrol: in action against German destroyers off Ushant early a.m. 9th: in action against U-boat 24th: damaged in action against German minesweepers off St Malo 28th

FAULKNOR   HM - left Solent (Anchorage 31/f6) 5th, arrived Juno 6th (Assault Convoy J1 minesweeper escort) and provided gunfire support: returned to Solent where arrived 1635 6th: carried General Montgomery to Juno 6th/7th: carried First Lord of the Admiralty to visit Eastern Task Force area 24th

FERNIE   HM (Hunt class) - left Solent 1530 6th, arrived Eastern Task Force area 7th (Convoy EWC1B escort)

FITCH   US - left Plymouth 5th, arrived Utah 6th (Assault Convoy U2B escort) and provided gunfire support

FORESTER   HM - left Thames 6th, arrived Eastern Task Force area 7th (Convoy ETP1 escort)

FORREST   US - left Plymouth 5th as reserve flagship, arrived Utah (Assault Convoy U1A escort) and subjected to enemy gunfire 0534 6th which returned: subjected to heavy gunfire 24th

FRANKFORD   US - left Weymouth Bay 5th, arrived Omaha 6th (Assault Convoy O1 escort) and provided gunfire support

FURY   HM - left Solent (Anchorage 31/f7) 5th, arrived Juno 6th (Assault Convoy J1 minesweeper escort) and provided gunfire support: damaged by mine at Gold 1040 21st, drifted ashore when tow parted in gale 0130 22nd, 0140 caught fire, tug BLACK ROCK alongside. *[Salved but not repaired]*

GARTH   HM (Hunt class) - left Thames 6th, arrived Eastern Task Force area 7th (Convoy L5/ETM1 escort)

GHERARDI   US - left Belfast Lough 3rd, via Weymouth Bay (to escort EREBUS), arrived Utah 6th (Assault Convoy U1A escort)

GLAISDALE   Norwegian (Hunt class) - left Solent (Anchorage 4/a6) 5th, arrived Juno 6th (Assault Convoy J10 escort) and provided gunfire support: 1824 23rd superficially damaged by mine in Sword area, towed to Mulberry B by SALVEDA, left 1230 24th using port engine and in tow of tug FREEDOM for Solent where anchored 2303 same day, then Immingham where arrived 1215 27th

GLENNON   US - left Belfast Lough 3rd, arrived Utah 6th (Assault Convoy U1A escort): damaged by mine 0806 8th and grounded by stern at Utah: hit by gunfire 10th and sank 2055 same day

GRENVILLE   HM - left Clyde 1130 3rd, arrived Gold 6th (Bombarding Force K/Assault Convoy G12 escort): grounded off Arromanches 6th, arrived Solent 7th to re-ammunition

HAIDA   Canadian - left Plymouth on patrol (Hurd Deep area) 5th: in action against German destroyers off Ushant early a.m. 9th: sank U-boat 24th

HAMBLEDON   HM (Hunt class) - left Solent (Anchorage 4/a5) 5th, arrived Gold 6th (Assault Convoy G16 escort): in action against E-boats night of 6th/7th

HAMBLETON   US - left Falmouth 5th, arrived Western Task Force area 6th (Follow-up Convoy B3/U4/ECL1 escort)

HARDING   US - left Weymouth Bay 5th, arrived Omaha 6th (Assault Convoy O1 escort) and provided gunfire support: struck submerged object and damaged propellers 8th

HERNDON   US - left Belfast Lough 3rd, arrived Utah 6th (Assault Convoy U1A escort): sent to assist MEREDITH 8th

HOBSON   US - left Plymouth, via Tor Bay, arrived Utah 6th (Assault Convoy U1A escort) and provided gunfire support: returned to Weymouth Bay 7th

HOLDERNESS   HM (Hunt class) - left Thames 24th for beach-head as convoy escort

HURON   Canadian - left Plymouth on patrol (Hurd Deep area) 5th: in action against German destroyers off Ushant early a.m. 9th and against German minesweepers off St Malo 28th

IMPULSIVE   HM - left Solent (Anchorage 28/a7) 1635 5th for Sword

ISIS   HM - left Solent (Anchorage 28/a8), left Spithead Gate 1230 6th, arrived Sword same day (PRINS ALBERT and PRINCESS MARGARET escort)

J. FRED TALBOTT   US - reported at Omaha as personnel vessel 13th

JAVELIN   HM - ex Plymouth on patrol: in action against German destroyers off Ushant early a.m. 9th

JEFFERS   US - left Belfast Lough 3rd, arrived Utah 6th (Assault Convoy U1A escort): reserve gunfire support vessel: superficially damaged in after engine room by gunfire 2000 7th

JERVIS   HM - left Solent (Anchorage 3N/a1) 1900 5th, arrived Gold 6th (Assault Convoy G9 escort): bows buckled when vessel blown against her in Eastern Task Force area approx 19th

JOUETT   US - convoy escort: left Omaha for Clyde 18th

KELVIN   HM - left Solent (Anchorage 28/a4), left Spithead Gate 2130 5th, arrived Sword 6th (Assault Convoy S7 escort): left Portsmouth 0830 12th carrying Prime Minister Winston Churchill on a day visit, arriving Juno 1200: returned 2100

KEMPENFELT   HM - left Solent (Anchorage 31/f1) 2135 5th, arrived Juno 0608 6th (Assault Convoy J10 escort): gunfire support vessel

KEPPEL   HM - left Solent 6th, arrived Eastern Task Force area 7th (Convoy EWC1A escort)

KRAKOWIAK   Polish (Hunt class) - left Solent (Anchorage 4/a1) 5th, arrived Gold 6th (Assault Convoy G1 minesweeper escort): returned to Solent where arrived 7th

LA COMBATTANTE   French (Hunt class) - left Solent (Anchorage 4/a7) 5th, arrived Juno 6th (Assault Convoy J9 escort) and provided gunfire support: carried General de Gaulle from Portsmouth to Eastern Task Force area, arrived 1245 14th, left 0530 15th

LAFFEY   US - left Plymouth 5th, arrived Utah 6th (Assault Convoy U2A2 escort): slightly damaged by gunfire during Cherbourg bombardment 25th

MACKAY   HM - left Thames 7th, arrived Eastern Task Force area 8th (Convoy ETM2 escort)

McCOOK   US - left Weymouth Bay 1130 5th, arrived Omaha 6th (minesweeper escort) and provided gunfire support

MELBREAK   HM (Hunt class) - left Weymouth Bay 5th, arrived Omaha 6th (Assault Force O) and provided gunfire support: in action against E-boats night 12th/13th

MENDIP   HM (Hunt class) - left Milford Haven 4th, left Bristol Channel 5th, arrived Omaha 7th (Convoy EBP1 escort): rescued survivors from SUSAN B. ANTHONY 7th

MEREDITH   US - left Plymouth, via Tor Bay, arrived Utah 6th (Assault Convoy U3 escort): damaged by air attack approx 0230 8th, broke in two and sank 1015 9th en route to being planted as a navigational mark

MEYNELL   HM (Hunt class) - left Thames 6th, arrived Eastern Task Force area 7th (Convoy L5/ETM1 escort)

MIDDLETON   HM (Hunt class) - left Solent (Anchorage 26N/a2) 1610 5th, arrived Sword 6th (Assault Convoy S2 minesweeper escort): in action against E-boats night 22nd/23rd

MONTROSE   HM - left Harwich 5th, arrived Eastern Task Force area 6th (Follow-up Convoy L4 escort)

MURPHY   US - left Belfast Lough 3rd, arrived Omaha 6th (Assault Convoy O1 escort): reserve gunfire support vessel

NELSON   US - arrived Omaha 6th (Assault Convoy O1 escort): reserve gunfire support vessel: stern blown off by E-boat *[S138]* torpedo in Omaha area 12th: towed from Solent to Londonderry early July

OBEDIENT   HM - left Sheerness 4th, left Thames on patrol (eastern English Channel) 5th: in action against E-boats 0130 8th

O'BRIEN   US - left Plymouth, via Tor Bay, arrived Utah 6th (Assault Convoy U1B escort) and allocated to Omaha for fire support: damaged by gunfire during Cherbourg bombardment 25th

OFFA   HM - left Solent (Anchorage 3N/a9) on patrol (on western flank of assault forces) 5th

ONSLAUGHT   HM - left Solent (Anchorage 3N/a7) on patrol (on western flank of assault forces) 5th: in action against U-boat 0742 29th

ONSLOW   HM - left Solent (Anchorage 3N/a6) on patrol (on western flank of assault forces) 5th: slightly damaged by bomb near miss night 6th/7th: in action against E-boats night 12th/13th: slightly damaged below waterline by aerial torpedo attack 2330 18th

OPPORTUNE   HM - left Sheerness 4th, left Thames on patrol (eastern English Channel) 5th: covered diversionary operation in the Strait of Dover 6th

ORIBI   HM - left Solent (Anchorage 3N/a8) on patrol (western flank of assault forces) 5th

ORWELL   HM - ex Sheerness, left Thames on patrol (eastern English Channel) 5th

PIORUN   Polish - ex Plymouth on patrol: in action against German destroyers off Ushant early a.m. 9th: slightly damaged in action against German minesweepers which were sunk or damaged SW of Jersey early a.m. 14th

PLUNKETT   US - left Belfast Lough 3rd, arrived Omaha 6th (Assault Convoy O1 escort): reserve gunfire support vessel: having failed to receive an answer to her challenge, vessel opened fire on and hit British cable ship MONARCH 13th

PYTCHLEY   HM (Hunt class) - left Solent (Anchorage 4/a2) 5th, arrived Gold 6th (Assault Convoy G2 minesweeper escort): assisted DINARD 7th

QUORN   HM (Hunt class) - left Thames 6th, arrived Eastern Task Force area 7th (Convoy ETP1 escort)

RODMAN   US - left Plymouth 5th, arrived Western Task Force area 6th (Follow-up Convoy B1 escort)

SATTERLEE   US - left Weymouth Bay 5th, arrived Omaha 6th (minesweeper escort) and provided gunfire support

SAUMAREZ   HM - left Clyde 2nd, arrived Sword 6th (Bombarding Force D/Assault Convoy S6 escort): slightly damaged by mine 2116 18th

SAVAGE   HM - ex Sheerness, left Thames on patrol (eastern English Channel) 5th

SCORPION   HM - left Solent (Anchorage 28/a3) 1330 5th, arrived Sword 6th (Assault Convoy S1 minesweeper escort): carried Admiral Stark (Commander US Naval Forces Europe) from Portsmouth to Western Task Force area 14th

SCOURGE leaving Spithead on 16th June, 1944. [IWM A24198]

SCOURGE   HM - left Solent (Anchorage 28/a1) 1530 5th, arrived Sword 6th (Assault Convoy S2 minesweeper escort)

SERAPIS   HM - left Solent (Anchorage 28/a2) 1530 5th, arrived Sword 6th (Assault Convoy S2 minesweeper escort): returned to Solent 7th

SHUBRICK   US - left Belfast Lough 3rd, arrived Utah 6th (Assault Convoy U1A escort) and provided gunfire support: returned to Weymouth Bay 7th

SIOUX   Canadian - left Solent (Anchorage 31/f5) 5th, arrived Juno 6th (Assault Convoy J2 minesweeper escort) and provided gunfire support

SLAZAK   Polish (Hunt class) - left Solent (Anchorage 26N/a3) 5th, arrived Sword 6th (Assault Convoy S2 minesweeper escort): damaged by grounding 11th

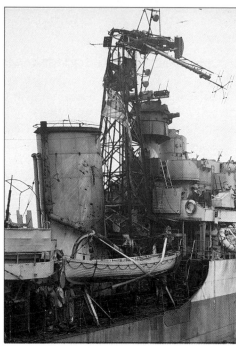

TARTAR on 10th June, 1944, with battle damage to mast and splinter holes in forward funnel.
[IWM A23985]

SOMERS   US - arrived Clyde 2200 1st en route to beach-head (convoy escort)

SOUTHDOWN   HM (Hunt class) - left Thames 7th, arrived Eastern Task Force area 8th (Convoy ETM2 escort)

STEVENSTONE   HM (Hunt class) - left Solent (Anchorage 4/a8) 2045 5th, arrived Juno 6th (Assault Convoy J9 escort) and provided gunfire support: returned to Portsmouth harbour where arrived 2345 6th: in action against E-boats night 22nd/23rd

STORD   Norwegian - left Clyde 2nd, arrived Sword 6th (Bombarding Force D/Assault Convoy S6 escort)

SVENNER   Norwegian - left Clyde 2nd for Sword (Bombarding Force D/Assault Convoy S6 escort) but sunk by torpedo boats *[JAGUAR, MOWE and T24]* 12 miles west of Le Havre 0535 6th

SWIFT   HM - left Clyde 2nd, arrived Sword 6th (Bombarding Force D/Assault Convoy S6 escort): 0710 24th struck mine which broke ship's back in Sword area and sank her one hour later

TALYBONT   HM (Hunt class) - left Weymouth Bay 5th, arrived Omaha 6th (Assault Force O) and provided gunfire support: in action against E-boats night 11th/12th: splinter damaged by gunfire early a.m. 17th

TANATSIDE   HM (Hunt class) - left Weymouth Bay 5th, arrived Omaha 6th (Assault Force O) and provided gunfire support: attacked two E-boats 0108 26th

TARTAR   HM - ex Plymouth on patrol (Hurd Deep area) 5th/6th: suffered and inflicted damage in action against German destroyers off Ushant early a.m 9th

THOMPSON   US - left Weymouth Bay 5th as reserve flagship, arrived Omaha 6th (Assault Convoy O1 escort) and provided gunfire support: carried Supreme Commander, General Eisenhower, and Admiral King on visit to beach-head 12th

ULSTER   HM - left Clyde 1100 3rd, arrived Gold 6th (Bombarding Force E/Assault Convoy G14 escort): damaged propeller shaft on grounding 9th: left Solent 0545 20th in tow of tug ABEILLE No. 21 for Cardiff where arrived 23rd

ULYSSES   HM - left Solent (Anchorage 3N/a3) 5th, arrived Gold 6th (Assault Convoy G9 escort)

UNDAUNTED   HM - left Solent (Anchorage 3N/a5) 5th, arrived Gold 6th (Assault Convoy G10 escort): carried Admiral Ramsay from beach-head to Portsmouth 7th

UNDINE   HM - left Clyde 1100 3rd, arrived Gold 6th (Bombarding Force K/Assault Convoy G12 escort)

URANIA   HM - left Solent (Anchorage 3N/a2) 5th, arrived Gold 6th (Assault Convoy G9 escort)

URCHIN   HM - left Clyde 1845 2nd, arrived Gold 6th (Bombarding Force E/Assault Convoy G14 escort)

URSA   HM - left Solent (Anchorage 3N/a4) 5th, arrived Gold 6th (Assault Convoy G10 escort)

VANQUISHER   HM - arrived Clyde 2nd (assigned as Convoy EBM3 escort ETA Western Task Force area 8th)

VENUS   HM - left Solent (Anchorage 31/f2) 5th, arrived Juno 6th (Assault Convoy J9 escort) and provided gunfire support

VERSATILE   HM - left Solent (Anchorage 22/e2) 1655 5th, arrived Juno 6th (Assault Convoy J14 escort)

VERULAM   HM - left Solent (Anchorage 28/a6), left Spithead Gate 2130 5th, arrived Sword 6th (Assault Convoy S7 escort): RAMILLIES escort to Solent 6th/7th

VESPER   HM - left Weymouth Bay 5th, arrived Omaha 6th (Assault Convoy O2 escort)

VIDETTE   HM - left Weymouth Bay 5th, arrived Omaha 6th (Assault Convoy O2 escort): in action against E-boats night of 12th/13th

VIGILANT   HM - left Solent (Anchorage 31/f3) 5th, arrived Juno 6th (Assault Convoy J2 minesweeper escort) and provided gunfire support

VIMY   HM - left Falmouth 5th, arrived Western Task Force area 6th (Follow-up Convoy B3/U4/ECL1 escort)

VIRAGO   HM - left Solent (Anchorage 28/a5), left Spithead Gate 2130 5th, arrived Sword 6th (Assault Convoy S7 escort)

VIVACIOUS   HM - left Harwich 5th, arrived Eastern Task Force area 6th (Follow-up Convoy L2 escort)

VOLUNTEER   HM - left Falmouth 5th, arrived Western Task Force area 6th (Follow-up Convoy B3/U4/ECL1 escort)

WALKE   US - left Plymouth 5th, arrived Utah 6th (Assault Convoy U2A1 escort): subjected to heavy gunfire 24th

WALKER   HM - left Milford Haven (assigned as Convoy EBC2Z escort ETA Western Task Force area 8th)

WALPOLE   HM - left Thames 8th, arrived Eastern Task Force area 9th (Convoy ETC3 escort)

WANDERER   HM - left Milford Haven (assigned as Convoy EBM2 escort ETA Western Task Force area 7th): shot down an enemy aircraft 10th

WATCHMAN   HM - left Milford Haven 5th, en route to Western Task Force area (as Convoy EBC3 escort) in action against E-boats 0245 9th

WENSLEYDALE   HM (Hunt class) - left Plymouth anchorage, arrived Western Task Force area 6th (Follow-up Convoy B1 escort): in action against E-boats nights 10th/11th and 12th/13th

WESTCOTT   HM - left Clyde 3rd (RODNEY escort)

WHITEHALL   HM - left Milford Haven 7th (assigned as Convoy EBC4 escort ETA Western Task Force area 10th)

WHITSHED   HM - left Harwich 5th, arrived Eastern Task Force area 6th (Follow-up Convoy L4 escort)

WINDSOR   HM - ex Thames (assigned as Convoy ETC2Y escort ETA Eastern Task Force area 7th)

WRESTLER   HM - left Solent (Anchorage 22/e1) 1350 5th, arrived Juno 6th (Assault Convoy J7 escort): damaged by mine 0637 6th, left 0845 6th under tow for Solent where arrived 2350 same day. *[Not repaired]*

Section B4 - SLOOPS, FRIGATES, US DESTROYER ESCORTS, CORVETTES, ANTI-SUBMARINE (A/S) TRAWLERS, STEAM GUNBOATS AND COASTAL FORCES

These vessels were assigned duties as escorts, accompanying convoys in British coastal waters and across the Channel, and in connection with coastal forces' operations. (All dates are June 1944 unless otherwise stated.)

HM Sloops

CRANE, **HART**, **HIND** (Assault Convoy G3 escort), **KITE**, **LAPWING**, **LARK**, **LONDONDERRY** (slightly damaged in collision 7th), **MAGPIE** (Assault Convoy G4 escort), **PELICAN**, **REDPOLE** (Assault Convoy G5 escort), **ROCHESTER** (under repair at Plymouth until 7th), **SCARBOROUGH**, **STORK** (Assault Convoy S9 escort replacing WOODCOCK), **WHIMBREL**. (**CYGNET** withdrawn mid May: **WOODCOCK** arrived Humber 6th for repairs after 27th May collision with VENUS)

HM Frigates

BULLEN (HMS NELSON escort ex Milford Haven), **CHELMER**, **CUBITT**, **CURZON**, **DAKINS**, **DEVERON**, **DUFF** (on patrol 5th/6th on western flank of assault forces: became coastal forces control ship 8th), **EKINS**, **GOODALL** (HMS NELSON escort ex Milford Haven), **HALSTED** (bows blown off in E-boat torpedo attack 0315 11th, surviving part arrived Solent in tow 12th *[Not repaired]*), **HARGOOD**, **HOLMES** (Bombarding Force D/Assault Convoy S6 escort ex Clyde), **HOTHAM** (on patrol on western flank of assault forces 5th/6th: rescued survivors from MAID OF ORLEANS 28th), **NARBROUGH**, **RETALICK** (on patrol on western flank of assault forces 5th/6th as coastal forces control ship: in action against E-boats night of 6th/7th: sent to rescue LST survivors from Convoy ECM1P after E-boat attack 9th), **RIOU** (RODNEY escort ex Clyde), **ROWLEY** (Bombarding Force D/Assault Convoy S6 escort ex Clyde), **RUPERT**, **SEYMOUR** (became coastal forces control ship 8th), **SPRAGGE**, **STAYNER** (on

HM frigate STAYNER.
[IWM A24049]

The French frigate LA SURPRISE escorting tank landing ships. [IWM A23902]

patrol on western flank of assault forces 5th/6th as coastal forces control ship: near missed by bomb night of 6th/7th: in action against E-boats 0320 8th: in action against U-boat night of 26th/27th), **STOCKHAM, STRULE, TAVY, THORNBROUGH** (on patrol on eastern flank of assault forces 5th/6th), **TORRINGTON** (Assault Convoy S11 escort: became coastal forces control ship 8th), **TROLLOPE** (on patrol on eastern flank of assault forces 5th/6th: in action against E-boats night of 10th/11th), **TYLER, WALDEGRAVE, WHITAKER**

French Frigates

L'AVENTURE (Assault Convoy O2 escort), **LA DECOUVERTE** (Assault Convoy G11 escort), **LA SURPRISE** (Assault Convoy G18 escort: port propeller shaft broken by mine at Omaha 20th, towed to Solent by ARIKARA 21st then to Pembroke), **L'ESCARMOUCHE** (Assault Convoy O2 escort)

US Destroyer Escorts

AMESBURY (Force O escort ex Belfast), **BATES** (Force U escort), **BLESSMAN** (Force O escort ex Belfast), **BORUM** (Assault Convoy O2 escort), **BUNCH** (Force U escort), **MALOY** (Flagship, Force B ex Plymouth), **RICH** (Force U escort: disintegrated after striking three mines while assisting GLENNON 0850 8th)

HM Corvettes

ABELIA, ARMERIA (damaged aft by torpedo night of 11th/12th), **AZALEA, BALSAM** (towed SOLITAIRE 19th), **BLUEBELL, BORAGE, BURDOCK** (Assault Convoy G13 escort), **BUTTERCUP, CAMELLIA, CAMPANULA** (Assault Convoy G17 escort: carried out 'PLUTO' operational reconnaissance 8th), **CELANDINE, CHARLOCK, CLARKIA** (Assault Convoy J15 escort: sent to assist LCT 1038 6th), **CLEMATIS, CLOVER** (Assault Convoy S12 escort), **DAHLIA, DIANELLA, DIANTHUS, GENTIAN, GERANIUM, GODETIA, HEATHER, HONEYSUCKLE, KINGCUP, LAVENDER** (Assault Convoy S14B escort), **LOOSESTRIFE** (grounded at Harwich 29th May), **MIGNONETTE, NARCISSUS, NASTURTIUM** (left Oban with Corncobs), **ORCHIS, OXLIP, PENNYWORT** (Assault Convoy S15 escort), **PETUNIA** (Assault Convoy J15 escort), **PINK** (Assault Convoy J15 escort: badly damaged aft by U-boat *[U-988]* torpedo 1600 27th and towed to Solent by BEAGLE *[Not repaired]*), **POPPY, POTENTILLA, PRIMROSE, PUFFIN, RHODODENDRON, STARWORT, STATICE, SUNFLOWER, SWEETBRIAR, VERVAIN, WALLFLOWER** (delayed undergoing repairs at Sheerness until 10th)

Canadian Corvettes

ALBERNI (damaged by gunfire 14th), **BADDECK** (COURBET escort to Mulberry: in action against E-boats 0110 13th), **CALGARY** (damaged in collision with a Mulberry Phoenix off Selsey 6th), **CAMROSE** (COURBET escort to Mulberry: in action against E-boats 0110 13th), **DRUMHELLER** (left Forth 23rd May with Corncobs), **KITCHENER, LINDSAY** (in action against E-boats 9th), **LOUISBURG** (left Forth 23rd May with Corncobs), **LUNENBURG, MAYFLOWER** (left Forth 23rd May with Corncobs), **MIMICO, MOOSEJAW, PORT ARTHUR, PRESCOTT, REGINA, RIMOUSKI** (left Forth 23rd May with Corncobs), **SUMMERSIDE, TRENTONIAN** (left Oban with Corncobs: escorted MONARCH 13th), **WOODSTOCK**

French Corvettes

ACONIT (Assault Convoy U3 escort), **COMMANDANT D'ESTIENNE D'ORVES, RENONCULE** (Assault Convoy U3 escort), **ROSELYS**

Greek Corvettes

KRIEZIS (Assault Convoy G17 escort), **TOMPAZIS** (Assault Convoy G13 escort)

Norwegian Corvettes

ACANTHUS (in action against U-boat 29th), **EGLANTINE, ROSE**

HM (Anti-Submarine) Trawlers

ACACIA, ANNET, BERN, BIRCH, BOMBARDIER (Assault Convoy G5 escort), **BRESSAY, CALDY** (assisted JAMES A. FARRELL 29th), **CAMBRIDGESHIRE, COLL, CORNELIAN, DAMSAY, DARTHEMA** (towed midget submarine X20 towards French coast 2nd/3rd then, after escorting Assault Convoy J14, towed X20 back to Portsmouth 6th), **DERBY COUNTY, ELLESMERE, FIARAY, FLINT** (Assault Convoy U3 escort), **FOULNESS, FUSILIER** (Assault Convoy G11 escort), **GAIRSAY, GANILLY** (in action against E-boats 9th), **GATESHEAD, GRASSHOLM, GRENADIER** (Assault Convoy G7 escort: shot down an enemy aircraft, parts of which hit ship 0110 7th), **GRIMSBY TOWN, GWEAL, HERSCHELL, HUDDERSFIELD TOWN, HUGH WALPOLE** (Assault Convoy S14A escort), **KINGSTON ANDALUSITE, KINGSTON CHRYSOBERYL, LANCER** (Assault Convoy G8 escort), **LINCOLNSHIRE, LINDISFARNE, LORD AUSTIN** (Assault Convoy J16 escort: near missed 2345 18th: lost port propeller 20th: 0555 24th struck mine, settled by the stern and sank in 10 minutes), **LORD ESSENDON, LORD MIDDLETON** (failed to sail from Exmouth with Convoy UB3 as intended), **LORD STANHOPE, LORD WAKEFIELD, NEAVE, NORTHERN FOAM** (Assault Convoy J15 escort), **NORTHERN GEM** (Assault Convoy S13 escort), **NORTHERN GIFT** (Assault Convoy S13 escort), **NORTHERN PRIDE** (Assault Convoy J15 escort: in action against E-boats night 22nd/23rd), **NORTHERN REWARD** (Assault Convoy S14A escort), **NORTHERN SKY** (Assault Convoy S4 escort), **NORTHERN SPRAY** (Assault Convoy J16 escort), **NORTHERN SUN** (Assault Convoy J16 escort), **NORTHERN WAVE** (Assault Convoy S10 escort), **OLVINA, PEARL, QUADRILLE, RUBY, SAPPER** (towed midget submarine X23 towards French coast 2nd/3rd then escorted Assault Convoy G6), **SCALPAY** (in action against E-boats 9th), **SKOMER, SKYE, STEEPHOLM, SWITHA** (took off medical staff firstly from DINARD then from ST JULIEN 7th), **TEXADA** (Assault Convoy U3 escort), **ULVA, VELETA** (Assault Convoy J16 escort replacing LORD MIDDLETON: towed drifting LCP 229 to Sword 6th), **VICTRIX** (Assault Convoy G13 escort)

Dutch Trawler

EN AVANT (Assault Convoy S10 escort then towed midget submarine X23 back to Portsmouth 6th)

French Trawlers as HM Anti-Submarine Vessels

ASIE, LA NANTAISE, NOTRE DAME DE FRANCE

HM trawler TEXADA. [IWM A27945]

HM Steam Gunboats

All, except GREY OWL, left Portland for Omaha 5th [Assault Convoy 03]

GREY FOX, **GREY GOOSE**, **GREY OWL** (under repair at Portsmouth following 25th May collision with GREY SEAL), **GREY SEAL**, **GREY SHARK**, **GREY WOLF** (storm damaged 21st)

HM steam gunboat GREY GOOSE in 1942. [Maritime Photo Library]

MTBs returning from patrol on 13th June, 1944. [IWM A24047]

Assigned Motor Gunboats

MGB 312, 316, 317, 324, 326, 330

Assigned Motor Torpedo Boats

MTB 24, 25, 83, 88, 93, 205-212, 223-225, 232-234, 238, 244-257, 347, 353, 354, 358, 359, 361, 362, 412-416, 430, 431, 434, 447-454, 459-466, 478, 481, 608, 611, 613-617, 621, 624, 628-630, 632, 650, 652, 664, 668, 672, 673, 676-680, 682, 689-695, 697-707, 710, 713, 714, 716, 717, 719-721, 724-728, 730, 735, 736, 738, 739, 742-746, 748, 749, 773

Assigned Motor Launches

ML 100-102, 104-107, 110, 112-114, 116-120, 122-125, 131, 136-143, 146, 147, 150, 151, 153-155, 157, 159, 163, 171, 179-187, 189-191, 193-198, 200-208, 212, 214, 217, 220, 222, 224, 230, 233, 236, 243, 245-248, 250, 252, 254, 255, 257, 259, 269, 275, 276, 286, 291-293, 297, 300, 303, 304, 309, 343-347, 442, 445, 448, 450, 452, 454, 464-467, 473, 488, 490, 491, 571, 572, 588, 589, 591, 594, 596-599, 901-905, 907, 908

Assigned Harbour Defence Motor Launches

HDML 1001, 1009, 1013, 1021, 1025, 1027, 1033-1035, 1053, 1055, 1056, 1060, 1081, 1085, 1091, 1279, 1295, 1309, 1379, 1382, 1383, 1387, 1389-1393, 1396, 1403, 1405, 1407-1410, 1413, 1415-1417, 1419, 1421, 1422

Assigned US (Submarine Chaser) Escorts

PC 484, 552, 553, 564-568, 617-619, 1176, 1225, 1232, 1233, 1252, 1261-1263, 1322, 1342

SC 1282, 1290, 1291, 1301, 1307, 1308, 1330, 1332, 1334, 1353, 1354, 1358, 1361

Section B5 - ANTI-SUBMARINE SCREEN

Anti-submarine (U-boat) groups, composed to a large extent of US Captain class frigates on Lend-Lease to Britain, were deployed in the approaches to the English Channel to prevent a concerted German attack cutting the vital Neptune convoy supply lines.

(All dates are June 1944 unless otherwise stated.)

HM US Escort Aircraft Carriers
ex Moelfre Bay

EMPEROR, **PURSUER**, **TRACKER** (in collision with TEME 0300 10th)

HM Destroyers
ex Plymouth

FAME (sank U-boat *[U-767]* 1756 18th), **HAVELOCK** (in action against U-boat *[U-767]* 18th), **HOTSPUR**, **ICARUS**, **INCONSTANT** (in action against U-boat *[U-767]* 18th), **SALADIN**, **SCIMITAR**, **SKATE**

Canadian Destroyers
ex Londonderry

CHAUDIERE, **GATINEAU** (in action against E-boats 26th), **KOOTENAY**, **OTTAWA**, **QU'APPELLE** (in action against U-boat 7th), **RESTIGOUCHE** (in action against U-boat 7th), **ST LAURENT**, **SASKATCHEWAN**, **SKEENA** (in action against U-boat 8th)

HM Sloops
left Moelfre Bay 5th

STARLING, **WILD GOOSE**, **WREN**

HM Frigates

AFFLECK (in action against U-boat 26th), **ANTIGUA**, **AYLMER**, **BALFOUR** (in action against U-boat 25th), **BENTLEY**, **BICKERTON** (in action against U-boat 15th: sank U-boat *[U-269]* 0416 25th), **BLACKWOOD** (in action against U-boat 12th: 1911 15th bows blown off by U-boat *[U-764]* torpedo, vessel sank whilst in tow 0410 16th), **BLIGH** (towed GOODSON to Portland 25th), **BRAITHWAITE**, **CAM** (temporarily joined 8th: stood by TEME 10th), **CAPEL**, **COOKE** (in action against U-boat 30th), **DOMETT** (in action against U-boat 30th), **DOMINICA**, **DUCKWORTH** (in action against U-boats 15th and 30th), **ESSINGTON** (in action against U-boats 12th and 30th), **GARLIES**, **GOODSON** (1316 25th damaged on port quarter by U-boat *[U-984]* torpedo and towed to Portland by BLIGH and to Belfast by tug ATA 172 *[Not repaired]*), **GORE**, **INGLIS**, **KEATS**, **LAWSON**, **LOCH FADA**, **LOCH KILLIN**, **LOCHY**, **LOUIS** (assigned 20th: damaged 24th), **MOORSOM**, **MOUNSEY**, **MOURNE** (blown up by U-boat *[U-767]* torpedo 1145 15th)

Canadian Frigates
ex Moelfre Bay

CAPE BRETON, **GROU**, **MATANE**, **MEON**, **OUTREMONT** (took TEME in tow 10th), **PORT COLBORNE** (damaged 29th), **ST JOHN**, **STORMONT**, **SWANSEA**, **TEME** (holed in collision with TRACKER 0300 10th), **WASKESIU**

Minesweepers at anchor in the Solent on 23rd June, 1944. [IWM]

Section B6 - MINESWEEPERS AND DANLAYERS

To clear pre-arranged approach channels for the assault fleet, a massive minesweeping operation was instituted. The first requirement of the minesweepers, with their accompanying danlayers to position flagged and lighted dan buoys, was to sweep the approach and fire support channels. On completion of this, the swept area was extended to the lowering positions, outer transport anchorages, the fire support area and the boat lanes to the beaches. It was intended that the flotillas subsequently work to a fortnightly schedule, with nine days in the assault area, three days replenishing in the Solent or at Portland and the other two on passage. Sweeping operations continued throughout June to counter the laying of new mines, often at night from the air. About 550 mines were accounted for during June in the Eastern Task Force area alone.

(All dates are June 1944 unless otherwise stated.)

1ST FLOTILLA   - left Solent (Anchorage 28) 1355 5th for Sword: streamed sweeps 1600 5th (Assault Convoy S1)

HM minesweepers **BRITOMART, GLEANER** (under repair until left Grimsby 7th, ETA beach-head 10th), **HALCYON, HARRIER** (damaged whilst oiling from RODNEY in Eastern Task Force area 19th), **HUSSAR, JASON, SALAMANDER, SEAGULL, SPEEDWELL.** (**SPEEDY** withdrawn mid May)

Attached danlayers - **ALEXANDER SCOTT, COLSAY** (lost propeller on grounding 19th, refloated 21st), **CRAFTSMAN, LORD ASHFIELD**

4TH FLOTILLA   - left Portland Harbour 0215 5th for Omaha

HM minesweepers **ALBURY, KELLETT** (holed forward on grounding in Swanage Bay 0129-1037 9th), **LYDD, PANGBOURNE, ROSS, SALTASH, SELKIRK, SUTTON.** (**ELGIN** under repair at Sheerness throughout June, following mine damage on 3rd May)

Attached danlayers - trawlers **FUDAY, NEIL SMITH, RIGHTO,** Canadian minesweeper **THUNDER**

6TH FLOTILLA - left Solent (Anchorage 1) 5th for Gold (Assault Convoy G1)

HM minesweepers **FRIENDSHIP, GOZO, LARNE, LIGHTFOOT, MELITA, PERSIAN** (damaged by mine 23rd and towed to Solent), **POSTILLION, VESTAL** (grounded 9th)

Attached danlayers - **COMMANDER EVANS** (left Plymouth 2nd to replace LORD MELCHETT which delayed Thames with engine trouble until 15th), **FAIRWAY** (damaged by mine 22nd), **HANNARAY, MILFORD PRINCE, SYLVANA**

7TH FLOTILLA - left Solent (Anchorage 29) 1145 5th for Juno: streamed sweeps 1833 5th (Assault Convoy J2)

HM minesweepers **FANCY, LENNOX, *PELORUS, PICKLE, PINCHER, PLUCKY, RECRUIT, RIFLEMAN**

Attached danlayers - **FARNE** (escorted WRESTLER to Solent 6th), **ST BARBE, STELLA LEONIS, STELLA RIGEL** (stood by WRESTLER 6th: damaged by mine at Juno 27th and towed by tug FARALLON 29th)

[* Vessel still afloat at Simonstown as PIETERMARITZBURG]

9TH FLOTILLA - left Solent (Anchorage 31) 1255 5th for Juno: streamed sweeps 1915 5th (Assault Convoy J1)

HM minesweepers **BANGOR, BLACKPOOL, BOSTON, BRIDLINGTON, BRIDPORT, EASTBOURNE, SIDMOUTH, TENBY**

Attached danlayers - **BRYHER, DALMATIA, IJUIN, SIGNA** (replacing QUIRPON)

14TH FLOTILLA - left Plymouth anchorage 5th for Utah (Assault Convoy UM2)[in sight of French coast from 1957 5th]

Canadian minesweepers **GEORGIAN, GUYSBOROUGH, KENORA**, HM minesweepers **POOLE, ROMNEY, RYE, SEAHAM, WHITEHAVEN**

Attached danlayers - **PETERHEAD, SIR GALAHAD, SIR LANCELOT, VEGREVILLE**

(GEORGIAN and VEGREVILLE switched roles early June)

PERSIAN (6th Flotilla) in April 1944. [IWM A22677]

PIQUE (40th Flotilla). [IWM A30787]

15TH FLOTILLA - left Dover 5th for Sword (Assault Convoy S2)

HM minesweepers **ARDROSSAN, BOOTLE, DUNBAR, FORT YORK, FRASERBURGH, LLANDUDNO, LYME REGIS, WORTHING**

Attached danlayers - **CALVAY, DOROTHY LAMBERT** (delayed by boiler defects), **JAMES LAY, NIBLICK**

16TH FLOTILLA - left Plymouth anchorage 5th for Utah

HM minesweepers **BEAUMARIS, DORNOCH, ILFRACOMBE** (damaged by mine 2026 21st), **PARRSBORO, QUALICUM, SHIPPIGAN, TADOUSSAC** (0032 9th hit by shell which did not explode), **WEDGEPORT**

Attached danlayers - **ARMANA** (replacing COMMANDER EVANS), **BLYTH, CANSO, KINGS GREY**

18TH FLOTILLA - left Solent (Anchorage 26S) 5th for Gold (Assault Convoy G2)

HM minesweepers **COCKATRICE, HOUND, HYDRA, LOYALTY, ONYX, ORESTES, RATTLESNAKE** (bottom corrugated by mine 15th), **READY**

Attached danlayers - **DOON, GILSAY, HORNBEAM, JUDE**

31ST FLOTILLA - left Weymouth Bay 0245 5th for Omaha

Canadian minesweepers **BLAIRMORE, CARAQUET, COWICHAN, FORT WILLIAM, MALPEQUE, MILLTOWN, MINAS, WASAGA**

Attached danlayers - **BAYFIELD, GREEN HOWARD, GUNNER, MULGRAVE**

40TH FLOTILLA - left Clyde 1850 2nd for Sword area: streamed sweeps 0245 6th (Assault Convoy S6)

HM US minesweepers **CATHERINE, CATO, GAZELLE, GORGON, GRECIAN, MAGIC, PIQUE** (rescued survivors from LAWFORD 8th: damaged by mine 25th) (**COMBATANT, STEADFAST** and **TATTOO** transferred out of Flotilla early June)

Attached danlayers - HM US minesweepers **CHAMOIS, CHANCE**

A SQUADRON   - ex Plymouth, left Tor Bay 5th for Utah

US minesweepers **AUK**, **BROADBILL**, **CHICKADEE**, **NUTHATCH** (damaged by mine 28th), **OSPREY** (struck mine 1759 5th, sank 1930 same day while in tow of tug BANNOCK), **PHEASANT** (damaged by mine 7th), **RAVEN** (lost one anchor 20th or 21st), **STAFF**, **SWIFT**, **THREAT**, **TIDE** (sunk by mine 0940 7th)

Assigned HM Magnetic Minesweepers

CONWAY CASTLE+, **COURTIER**, **GEORGETTE**, **NORTHCOATES**+, **PERDRANT**, **PROBE**, **PROCTOR**, **PROOF**, **PROWESS**, **SIR AGRAVAINE**+, **SIR GARETH**+, **SIR GERAINT**, **SIR KAYE**, **SIR LAMORAK**, **SIR TRISTRAM**+
(+ ordered to Plymouth 29th May)

Assigned Motor Minesweepers

MMS 6-8, 14, 17, 19, 22, 27-29, 31, 37, 40, 44, 45, 49, 55, 62, 71, 74, 75, 84, 86, 91, 110, 113, 115, 139, 165, 181-183, 186, 189, 205, 218, 219, 229, 247, 248, 251-253, 256, 257, 260, 261, 265, 266, 268, 274, 277-280, 288, 291, 293, 297, 301, 302, 305, 308, 1003, 1006-1011, 1037

BYMS 2001-2004, 2015, 2016, 2030, 2032, 2035, 2039, 2041, 2042, 2050, 2052, 2055, 2058, 2059, 2061, 2062, 2069, 2070, 2071, 2078, 2079, 2154-2157, 2167, 2173, 2182, 2202, 2205, 2206, 2210, 2211, 2233, 2252, 2255, 2256

YMS 231, 247, 304, 305, 346-352, 356, 358, 375, 377-382, 406

OSPREY (A Squadron).

Landing craft, gun (large) 1062 off the Juno beach-head, with TASAJERA, in the left background.

LBF (Landing Barge, Flak) **1-15** (for anti-aircraft defence)

LBV(2) (Landing Barge, Vehicle [Mark 2]) **1-55, 57-111, 113-133, 135-157, 159-181, 183-206, 208-217, 221-225, 227-232, 235-240** (for ferrying stores)

LCA(HR) (Landing Craft, Assault [Hedgerow]) **671, 686, 690, 708, 709, 712, 716, 719, 776, 829, 873, 874, 876, 880, 960-963, 965, 966, 968-970, 972, 976, 977, 1001, 1002, 1064, 1070-1072, 1101-1110, 1285-1287** (to project anti-mine bombs)

LCF(2)/(3)/(4) (Landing Craft, Flak [Marks 2, 3 and 4]) **1, 3, 5-7, 9, 11, 12, 18-22, 24-27, 29-39, 42** (for anti-aircraft and E-boat defence)

LCG(L)(3)/(4) (Landing Craft, Gun [Large][Marks 3 and 4]) **1-3, 5-7, 9-11, 13, 17, 18, 424, 426, 449, 680, 681, 687, 764, 811, 831, 893, 939, 1007, 1062** (for heavy gun support)

Landing craft, tank (rocket) 440 on 3rd June, 1944. [IWM B5263]

LCM(1)/(3) (Landing Craft, Mechanised [Marks 1 and 3]) **77, 114, 128, 138, 154, 164-166, 168, 171, 180, 184, 191, 193, 199, 202, 203, 216, 217, 223, 226, 229, 231, 236, 238-242, 244-251, 256, 262, 265-270, 274, 276, 281, 289, 290, 298, 303, 306-308, 311-314, 316-321, 330, 333-340, 342, 344-365, 368, 369, 372-374, 377-387, 407-409, 419-426, 431, 443, 444, 465, 524, 526, 530, 531, 535, 541, 557, 560, 561, 563, 573, 576, 577, 582, 587, 625, 627, 629, 940, 1050, 1051, 1053-1060, 1065, 1075, 1080, 1088, 1090, 1100, 1106, 1114, 1127, 1128, 1132, 1138, 1144-1146, 1161-1164, 1172, 1175, 1176, 1179, 1180, 1184, 1188-1193, 1196, 1197, 1200, 1201, 1208, 1212-1216, 1219-1222, 1224-1227, 1229, 1232-1236, 1239-1242, 1244-1246, 1277-1280, 1282, 1284, 1285, 1287-1290, 1292, 1293, 1296-1298, 1371, 1390-1393** (for ferrying duties)

LCP(SY) (Landing Craft, Personnel [Survey]) **139, 154, 177, 190, 201, 281, 289-292** (for hydrographic duties)

LCS(L)(1)/(2) (Landing Craft, Support [Large] [Marks 1 and 2]) **202-205, 251-260** (for gun support)

LCT(A) (Landing Craft, Tank [Armoured]) **2005, 2008-2010, 2012, 2014, 2037, 2039, 2042, 2043, 2048, 2052, 2120, 2121, 2123, 2124, 2191, 2225, 2227, 2228, 2233, 2236, 2238, 2262, 2263, 2266, 2273, 2275, 2282, 2283, 2291, 2301, 2309, 2310, 2334, 2345, 2402, 2426, 2428, 2432, 2433, 2442, 2453-2455, 2478, 2488, 2499** (carrying tanks which can fire during the assault)

LCT(R) (Landing Craft, Tank [Rocket]) **331, 334, 337, 359, 362, 363, 366-368, 378, 398, 405, 419, 423, 425, 434-440, 447, 448, 450, 452, 457, 458-460, 464, 473, 481-483** (fitted with rocket projectors)

Section B8 - MISCELLANEOUS VESSELS

APOLLO [IWM FL745]

NAME OF VESSEL   Tonnage/year of build, nationality (owner) of merchant ships, type - origin and/or assembly area, destination and convoy of first sailing: other information. (All dates are June 1944 unless otherwise stated.)

APOLLO   HM minelayer - laid mines off Ushant 9th-25th May: left Milford Haven 3rd, left Portsmouth Harbour (No.5 buoy) 0750 7th carrying General Eisenhower and Admiral Ramsay, arrived beach-head 1330 same day: damaged propeller on fouling bank 1612 7th so returned to Portsmouth on starboard engine, without distinguished passengers

CORONIA   227/35   Br excursion ship as HM despatch vessel - left Solent, ETA Gold 16th (Convoy ETC10W)

EASTWAY   HM US LSD (landing ship, dock) - arrived Portland 15th, left Solent 19th, ETA Juno same day (Convoy ETM13)

EASTWAY [IWM A20413]

FDT 13 in March 1944. [IWM A22529]

FDT 13 LST as HM Fighter Direction Tender - left Solent (Anchorage 20W), arrived 6th in position in the main shipping route to control allied fighter aircraft in that area (Assault Convoy G13F): returned 13th

FDT 216 LST as HM Fighter Direction Tender - left Portland, arrived Omaha 6th to control allied fighter aircraft in that area: damaged in collision with LST 523 7th; returned 15th for repairs after being damaged by relief vessel FDT 217

FDT 217 LST as HM Fighter Direction Tender - replaced FDT 216 mid May, left Solent (Anchorage 20W), arrived Eastern Task Force area 6th to control allied fighter aircraft in that area (Assault Convoy S13): withdrawn 23rd

MINNA 290/39 Br (Scottish Fishery Patrol) trawler - ex Falmouth, left, ETA Juno 29th (Convoy ETC21)

Motor Fishing Vessels included -

MFV 1034, 1067 (both intended for Convoy EWC1B ETA 7th)

NORTHWAY HM US LSD (landing ship, dock) - loaded at Solent anchorage, left Solent (Anchorage 5/a13) 0040 6th, arrived Juno 1755 same day to discharge a cargo of 46 loaded DUKWs [2½ ton 6-wheeled amphibious truck] (Force J4) (Follow-up Convoy L1): left 1940 6th

OCEANWAY HM US LSD (landing ship, dock) - left Portland Harbour 0610 6th, arrived Omaha 1530 same day to discharge 20 landing craft, each loaded with one tank (Follow-up Convoy B2): left 2200 same day for Portland where arrived 0705 7th

PLOVER HM minelayer - arrived Harwich 5th, on stand-by to reinforce the Sandiette Bank minefields

PRINCESS IRIS 2,683/17 Br (London & North Eastern Railway) train ferry TRAIN FERRY No.1 as HM LSS (landing ship, stern-chute) - ex Falmouth, left Solent for Juno end June

ROCKAWAY US seaplane carrier - arrived Solent 6th, left Solent, ETA beach-head 9th (Convoy ECP1W): in action against suspected U-boat contact 14th

TARANSAY HM examination vessel - left Solent, ETA Juno 26th (Convoy ETM17W)

PLOVER [IWM A13298]

PRINCESS IRIS in March 1946. [Wright & Logan]

Train Ferries assigned -

HAMPTON FERRY 2,839/34 Br (Southern Railway) - left Falmouth 1730 3rd July for Southampton

LAKEHURST 8,108/40 US SEATRAIN NEW JERSEY - left Belfast 22nd for Cardiff

SEATRAIN TEXAS 8,108/40 US - left Belfast 22nd, arrived Cardiff 24th

TWICKENHAM FERRY 2,839/34 Br (MoWT) ex-French - left Swansea Bay 19th, via Plymouth, for Southampton

Yachts assigned included -

ADVENTURESS (left Solent, ETA Gold 16th [Convoy ETC10W] as VHF radio link between northbound convoys and UK shore authorities)
ALTONA (for Juno)
ALVISTA (ex Poole)
CLARINDA (for Juno)
DIANA II (for Gold [Assault Convoy G9])
JUDITH (Force J)
LETNA (for Juno)
ST ADRIAN see Section B1
SEMITA (ex Poole)
SISTER ANNE (as despatch boat for Juno)
SWALLOW (for Juno)
THALABA (Force J)
THELAS (as landing barge HQ at Sword)

X20 HM midget submarine - left Portsmouth 2135 2nd: towed part of way by trawler DARTHEMA: acted as navigational marker at Sword: arrived back at Portsmouth 2320 6th again with DARTHEMA

X23 HM midget submarine - left Portsmouth 2nd: towed part of way by trawler SAPPER: acted as navigational marker at Juno: returned 6th with trawler EN AVANT

The yacht ADVENTURESS in 1941. [Wright & Logan]

PART C
OTHER VESSELS
Section C1 - ANTI-AIRCRAFT (Eagle) SHIPS

GOATFELL in May 1944. [Maritime Photo Library]

NAME OF VESSEL   Tonnage/year of build, nationality (owner) of merchant ships - origin and/or assembly area, destination and convoy of first sailing: other information. (All dates are June 1944 unless otherwise stated.)

DOUWE AUKES   Dutch minelayer as HM ship - left Solent (Anchorage 22/a9), arrived Port en Bessin 1800 7th (Convoy EWC1B)

GOATFELL   624/34   Br (Caledonian) passenger vessel CALEDONIA as HM ship - ex Solent (Anchorage 22/a2) for Western Task Force area (intended for Convoy EWC1A ETA 7th): returned 21st

GOLDEN EAGLE   793/09   Br (General Steam) excursion vessel as HM ship - left Solent (Anchorage 22/a1), arrived Port en Bessin 1800 7th (Convoy EWC1B)

RYDE   603/37   Br (Southern Railway) passenger vessel as HM ship - left Solent (Anchorage 22/a6) 1608 6th, ETA Western Task Force area 7th (intended for Convoy EWC1A): at Omaha 15th: returned 21st

SANDOWN   684/34   Br (Southern Railway) passenger vessel as HM ship - ex Weymouth Bay for Western Task Force area: became Mulberry A control vessel 11th: lost anchor at Omaha in gale 20th, taken in tow by tug CORMORANT

SCAWFELL   642/37   Br (Caledonian) passenger vessel JUPITER as HM ship - ex Weymouth Bay for Western Task Force area: became Mulberry A control vessel 11th

THAMES QUEEN   517/98   Br (New Medway) vessel as HM ship - left Solent (Anchorage 22/a7), arrived Eastern Task Force area 0830 7th (Convoy EWC1B): towed to Solent by tug EMPIRE LARCH 24th

WHIPPINGHAM   825/30   Br (Southern Railway) passenger vessel as HM ship - left Solent (Anchorage 22/a8), arrived Eastern Task Force area 0830 7th (Convoy EWC1B)

Blockships in the Western Task Force area with a US landing craft repair ship within the sheltered area. [IWM]

A fleet of elderly or damaged ships was assembled to be sunk in shallow water off each of the five beach-heads, to provide shelter for the smaller craft. The first contingent moved in three convoys, codenamed 'Corncobs', with I and II reaching the French coast between 1200 and 1400 on the 7th and III, consisting of the oldest or slowest vessels, arriving one day later. The ships had a 10lb demolition charge placed either side in each hold, three feet below the waterline and it normally took 20-25 minutes from the time of blowing the charges to the vessel settling on the bottom. The plan was for one ship to be scuttled or planted every 40 minutes. The ships' superstructure remained above the water-level enabling the accommodation to be utilised.

The shelters were named 'Gooseberries' and numbered 1-5 -

1 - situated off Utah, was laid during enemy gunfire and ended up somewhat out of line and with a gap

2 - off Omaha (Mulberry A), was planted too quickly with insufficient overlap and two gaps

3 - off Gold (Mulberry B), went according to plan except for one ship

4 - off Juno, was laid with the angle between the arms more acute than planned, providing a smaller area of lee than intended

5 - off Sword, was not laid as required with the result that it provided little protection against NE winds.

Gooseberries 3, 4 and 5 were finished on the 10th, one day earlier than 1 and 2. Gaps occurred in the originally-laid Gooseberries, partly as a result of gale damage, and additional blockships were therefore assigned as reinforcements, not all of which were in the event used.

NAME OF VESSEL   Tonnage/year of build, nationality (owner) of merchant ships, type - origin and/or assembly area, destination and convoy: other information. (All dates are June 1944 unless otherwise stated.)

AGHIOS SPYRIDON   3,338/05   Greek - ex Southampton, left Oban end May, left Poole Bay 1200 7th, arrived Gooseberry 3 8th (Corncob III): planted 2315 9th

ALYNBANK   5,151/25   Br (MoWT) - ex Liverpool, left Oban end May, left Poole Bay 1600 6th, arrived Gooseberry 3 1130 7th (Corncob I): was the first blockship to be planted, put into position 1300 7th but swung 124 degrees out of line on settling at 1407

ALYNBANK, stern to camera. [IWM]

ARTEMAS WARD   7,177/42   US Liberty type - ex Irish Sea, via Poole Bay, arrived Gooseberry 2 (Corncob)

AUDACIOUS   7,455/13   Panamanian - ex Irish Sea, via Poole Bay, arrived Gooseberry 2 (Corncob)

BAIALOIDE   6,476/14   Panamanian - ex Irish Sea, via Poole Bay, arrived Gooseberry 2 (Corncob)

BECHEVILLE   4,228/24   Br (MoWT) - ex Leith, left Oban end May, left Poole Bay 1600 6th, arrived Gooseberry 5 7th (Corncob I): planted 8th

BELGIQUE   4,606/02   Belgian - left Glasgow 22nd March, (switched with FORBIN end May) left Oban end May, via Poole Bay, for Gooseberry 4 (Corncob)

BENDORAN   5,567/10   Br (MoWT) - ex Manchester, left Oban end May, left Poole Bay 1600 6th, arrived Gooseberry 4 7th (Corncob I)

BENJAMIN CONTEE   7,176/42   US Liberty type - ex Irish Sea, via Poole Bay, arrived Gooseberry 1 (Corncob)

CENTURION   HM former battleship later target vessel - left Weymouth Bay, arrived Gooseberry 2 (Corncob III): planted 9th: started to break up in gale 21st

COURAGEOUS   7,573/18   US - ex Irish Sea, via Poole Bay, arrived Gooseberry 2 (Corncob): planted 8th

COURBET   Veteran French battleship - towed from Plymouth 21st May and from Weymouth Bay by GROWLER and SAMSONIA 7th, arrived Gooseberry 5 pm 8th: planted 9th

DAVID O. SAYLOR   4,826/43   US concrete vessel - ex Irish Sea, via Poole Bay, arrived Gooseberry 1 (Corncob)

DOVER HILL   5,815/18   Br (MoWT) - left Forth 17th April, left Oban end May, left Poole Bay 1600 6th, arrived Gooseberry 5 7th (Corncob I): planted 8th

DURBAN   HM cruiser - left Forth 23rd May, left Oban end May, left Poole Bay 1600 6th, arrived Gooseberry 5 7th (Corncob I): planted 9th, some injuries being caused by blast through hatches, vents and deck openings

ELSWICK PARK   4,188/20   Br (MoWT) - left Oban end May, left Poole Bay 1200 7th, arrived Gooseberry 3 8th (Corncob III): planted 1520 10th

EMPIRE BUNTING   6,448/19   US EELBECK as Br (MoWT) vessel - left Barry 21st March, left Oban end May, left Poole Bay 1600 6th, arrived Gooseberry 4 7th (Corncob I)

EMPIRE DEFIANCE   4,632/09   Italian ERICA as Br (MoWT) vessel - left Liverpool 7th April, left Oban end May, left Poole Bay 1600 6th, arrived Gooseberry 5 7th (Corncob I): planted 8th

EMPIRE FLAMINGO   5,207/20   US JOLEE as Br (MoWT) vessel - left Liverpool 16th April, left Oban end May, left Poole Bay 1600 6th, arrived Gooseberry 4 7th (Corncob I)

EMPIRE MOORHEN   5,617/19   US WEST TOTANT as Br (MoWT) vessel - left Glasgow 10th March, left Oban end May, left Poole Bay 1600 6th, arrived Gooseberry 4 7th (Corncob I)

EMPIRE TAMAR   6,561/07   Italian VERBANIA as Br (MoWT) vessel - left Glasgow 15th March, left Oban end May, left Poole Bay 1600 6th, arrived Gooseberry 5 7th (Corncob I): planted 8th

EMPIRE TANA   6,148/23   Italian CARSO as Br (MoWT) vessel - left Oban end May, left Poole Bay 1600 6th, arrived Gooseberry 5 7th (Corncob I): planted 8th

EMPIRE WATERHEN   6,004/20   US MANATEE as Br (MoWT) vessel - left Glasgow 3rd March, left Clyde 19th March, left Oban end May, left Poole Bay 1200 7th, arrived Gooseberry 4 8th (Corncob III)

FLIGHT-COMMAND   4,341/11   Panamanian - ex Irish Sea, via Poole Bay, arrived Gooseberry 2 (Corncob)

FLOWERGATE   5,156/11   Br (MoWT) - left Leith 15th April, left Forth, left Oban end May, left Poole Bay 1600 6th, arrived Gooseberry 3 1130 7th (Corncob I): planted 1305 9th

FORBIN   7,291/22   Br (MoWT) ex-French - (switched with BELGIQUE end May) left Oban end May, via Poole Bay, arrived Gooseberry 5 (Corncob): planted 8th

FORMIGNY   2,166/15   Br (MoWT) ex-French - ex Faslane, withdrawn from operation end May

GALVESTON   6,173/21   US - ex Irish Sea, via Poole Bay, arrived Gooseberry 2 (Corncob)

GEORGE S. WASSON   7,176/43   US Liberty type - ex Irish Sea, via Poole Bay, arrived Gooseberry 1 (Corncob)

GEORGE W. CHILDS   7,176/43   US Liberty type - ex Irish Sea, via Poole Bay, arrived Gooseberry 2 (Corncob)

GEORGIOS P.   4,052/03   Greek - ex Middlesbrough, left Oban end May, left Poole Bay 1600 6th, arrived Gooseberry 3 1130 7th (Corncob I): planted 2120 8th

INGMAN   3,169/07   Estonian LAKE HALLWIL as Br (MoWT) vessel - ex Leith, left Oban end May, via Poole Bay, arrived Gooseberry 3 8th (Corncob III)

INNERTON   5,276/19   Br (MoWT) - ex London, left Oban end May, left Poole Bay 1600 6th, arrived Gooseberry 3 1130 7th (Corncob I): planted 9th

JAMES IREDELL   7,177/42   US Liberty type - ex Irish Sea, via Poole Bay, arrived Gooseberry 2 (Corncob)

Blockships forming Gooseberry 3. [IWM]

JAMES W. MARSHALL   7,176/42   US Liberty type - ex Cardiff, via Poole Bay, arrived Gooseberry 2 (Corncob)

LYNGHAUG   2,829/19   Norwegian - arrived Forth 15th April, left Oban end May, left Poole Bay 1200 7th, arrived Gooseberry 3 8th (Corncob III): planted 10th

MANCHESTER SPINNER   4,767/18   Br (MoWT) - ex Manchester, left Oban end May, left Poole Bay 1600 6th, arrived Gooseberry 4 7th (Corncob I)

MARIPOSA   3,807/14   Br (MoWT) - ex Tyne, left Oban end May, left Poole Bay 1600 6th, arrived Gooseberry 4 7th (Corncob I)

MATT W. RANSOM   7,177/43   US Liberty type - ex Irish Sea, via Poole Bay, arrived Gooseberry 1 (Corncob)

MODLIN   3,569/06   Polish - left Oban end May, left Poole Bay 1600 6th, arrived Gooseberry 3 1130 7th (Corncob I): planted 1415 8th

NJEGOS   4,393/08   Br (MoWT) ex-Yugoslav - ex Liverpool, left Poole Bay 1200 7th, arrived Gooseberry 3 8th (Corncob III): planted 2218 8th

SUMATRA proceeding inshore at Sword.

OLAMBALA 4,815/01 Panamanian - ex Irish Sea, via Poole Bay, arrived Gooseberry 2 (Corncob)

PANOS 4,914/20 Br (MoWT) - left Manchester 6th April, left Oban end May, left Poole Bay 1600 6th, arrived Gooseberry 4 7th (Corncob I)

PARKLAAN 3,807/11 Dutch - left Middlesbrough 7th April, left Forth, left Oban end May, left Poole Bay 1600 6th, arrived Gooseberry 3 1130 7th (Corncob I): planted 1541 8th

POTTER 6,174/20 Panamanian - ex Irish Sea, via Poole Bay, arrived Gooseberry 2 (Corncob)

SALTERSGATE 3,940/24 Br (MoWT) - ex Leith, left Oban end May, left Poole Bay 1600 6th, arrived Gooseberry 3 1130 7th (Corncob I): planted 1110 8th in position originally assigned to ALYNBANK

SIREHEI 3,888/07 Norwegian - left Leith 11th April, left Forth, left Oban end May, left Poole Bay 1600 6th, arrived Gooseberry 3 1130 7th (Corncob I): planted 1230 10th

SUMATRA Dutch cruiser - ex Scapa, left Oban end May, left Poole Bay 1200 7th, arrived Gooseberry 5 8th (Corncob III): planted 9th

VERA RADCLIFFE 5,587/25 Br (MoWT) - ex Glasgow, left Oban end May, left Poole Bay 1600 6th, arrived Gooseberry 4 7th (Corncob I): Gooseberry 4 HQ established 11th

Part of Gooseberry 5 on 12th June, 1944, with SUMATRA in the centre and DURBAN beyond. [IWM A24055]

VICTORY SWORD 4,750/10 US - ex Irish Sea, via Poole Bay, arrived Gooseberry 1 (Corncob)

VINLAKE 3,938/13 CSIKOS as Br (MoWT) vessel - left Tyne 15th April, left Forth, left Oban end May, left Poole Bay 1200 7th, arrived Gooseberry 3 8th (Corncob III): planted 1128 9th

VITRUVIUS 4,826/43 US concrete vessel - ex Irish Sea, via Poole Bay, arrived Gooseberry 1 (Corncob)

WEST CHESWALD 5,711/19 US - ex Irish Sea, via Poole Bay, arrived Gooseberry 1 (Corncob)

WEST GRAMA 5,326/18 US - ex Irish Sea, via Poole Bay, arrived Gooseberry 2 (Corncob)

WEST HONAKER 5,428/20 US - ex Irish Sea, via Poole Bay, arrived Gooseberry 1 (Corncob III): en route damaged by aerial torpedo 0227 8th but completed voyage

WEST NOHNO 5,769/19 US - ex Irish Sea, via Poole Bay, arrived Gooseberry 1 (Corncob)

WILLIS A. SLATER 4,826/44 US concrete vessel - ex Irish Sea, via Poole Bay, arrived Gooseberry 1 (Corncob)

WILSCOX 5,861/19 US - ex Irish Sea, via Poole Bay, arrived Gooseberry 2 (Corncob)

WINHA 3,391/04 Br (MoWT) - ex Glasgow, left Oban end May, left Poole Bay 1200 7th, arrived Gooseberry 3 8th (Corncob III): planted 9th

Blockships being prepared at British ports on 24th June (G = Gooseberry)

ALCOA LEADER	5,041/19 US	- Newport (planted G2 13th July)
BOSWORTH	6,672/19 Br (MoWT)	- Glasgow (left 12th August for G3)
EMPIRE ADVOCATE	5,787/13 Br (MoWT)	- London then Forth (not used)
EMPIRE BITTERN	8,546/02 Br (MoWT)	- Liverpool (planted G3 23rd July)
EXFORD	4,969/19 US	- Liverpool (planted G2 26th July)
ILLINOIAN	6,473/18 US	- Glasgow (planted G2 28th July)
KELBERGEN	4,823/14 Dutch	- Greenock (not used)
KENTUCKIAN	5,200/10 US	- Barry (planted G2 12th July)
KOFRESI	4,934/20 US	- Penarth (planted G2 14th July)
LENA LUCKENBACH	5,238/20 US	- Tyne (planted G2 4th August)
MAYCREST	5,923/13 Br (Crest)	- Cardiff (left in tow 29th July, arrived G2 1st August)
NORFOLK	5,675/19 Norwegian	- Clyde (sunk by mine en route 20th July)

EMPIRE BITTERN [World Ship Society]

NORJERV	5,582/19 Norwegian	- Cardiff (planted G4 mid-July)
PARKHAVEN	4,803/20 Dutch	- London then Hull (left 21st July for G3)
PENNSYLVANIAN	5,191/13 US	- Glasgow (left 14th July)
PERSIER	5,382/18 Belgian	- Liverpool then Clyde (not used)
ROBIN GRAY	6,896/20 US	- Newport (planted G2 15th July)
SAHALE	5,028/19 US	- Hull (planted 24th July)
STANWELL	5,767/14 Br (MoWT)	- Swansea (planted G2 16th July)
WEST NILUS	5,495/20 US	- Cardiff (planted G2 16th July)

The Polish cruiser **DRAGON** was declared a total loss after being damaged at 0434 8th July: she was stripped of fittings but not of her main armament and planted at G4 about 23rd July.

Section C3 - BUOY-LAYING AND SURVEY SHIPS

NAME OF VESSEL   Tonnage/year of build, nationality (owner) of merchant ships, type - origin and/or assembly area, assignment: other information. (All dates are June 1944 unless otherwise stated.)

ALERT   793/19   Br (Trinity House) - left Solent (Anchorage 19E) 6th: 0810 16th struck mine when en route Gold to Cowes, while in tow vessel settled by stern and sank 0940 same day

ANDRE BLONDEL   French - loaded navigational buoys in Portsmouth Harbour, left Cowes (Anchorage 19E) 6th to join the minesweeping force

ASTRAL   HM survey ship - loaded navigational buoys in Portsmouth Harbour, left Solent (Anchorage 23N/1) 6th, joined 9th Minesweeping Flotilla 1300 7th to lay buoys

DISCOVERY II   1,036/29   Br (Falkland Islands) - left Solent (Anchorage 19E) 6th

FRANKLIN   HM survey ship - ex Scapa (in reserve): left for beach-head early July

GEORGES DE JOLI   French - loaded navigational buoys in Portsmouth Harbour, left Solent (Anchorage 19E) 6th to join the minesweeping force

GULNARE   HM survey ship - ex Solent for Mulberry A (intended for Convoy EWC1A ETA 7th) for survey duty

PATRICIA   1,116/38   Br (Trinity House) - left Solent (Anchorage 19E): laid navigational buoys 8th

SCOTT   HM survey vessel for blockships and Phoenix units and layer of positioning dan buoys - loaded navigational buoys in Portsmouth Harbour, left Solent (Anchorage 23N/2) 6th

WARDEN   828/29   Br (Trinity House) - left Solent (Anchorage 19E) 6th

Section C4 - CABLE VESSELS
for laying cross-Channel telephone connections.

NAME OF VESSEL   Tonnage/year of build, nationality (owner) of merchant ships - origin and/or assembly area, assignment: other information. (All dates are June 1944 unless otherwise stated.)

ALERT   941/18   Br (Postmaster General) - ex Thames via Solent, left Southbourne 0001 9th to land telephone line near Port en Bessin (ETA 2000 9th): returned to Solent 12th

EMPIRE FLAMINIAN   2,763/17   FLAMINIAN as Br (MoWT) cable store ship

IRIS   1,479/40   Br (Postmaster General) - left London 3rd, left Thames 5th, left Southbourne 0001 9th to land telephone line near Port en Bessin (ETA 2000 9th)

LESLIE   barge - ex Poole, left Southbourne 0001 9th to land telephone line near Port en Bessin (ETA 2000 9th)

MONARCH   1,150/16   Br (Postmaster General) - left Thames 8th, left Solent 0001 12th: in error, ship hit by gunfire from US destroyer PLUNKETT 0240 13th: towed to Portsmouth Harbour by tug EMPIRE BELLE

NORMAN   barge - ex Poole, left 0001 12th but towed back with engine trouble

ST MARGARETS   HM vessel - left Thames 5th, left Solent 0001 12th

Section C5 - COLLIERS

NAME OF VESSEL   Tonnage/year of build, nationality (owner) - origin and/or assembly area, destination and convoy of first sailing: other information. (All dates are June 1944 unless otherwise stated.)

ARY LENSEN   3,214/30   Br (Ary) - left Swansea Bay 20th, via Poole Bay, ETA Omaha 24th (Convoy EBC17)

BARON RUTHVEN   3,178/25   Br (Hogarth) - after loading, left London 4th, left Thames 0100 7th, ETA Gold 8th (Convoy ETC22)

BILTON   746/20   Br (Tyne-Tees) - after loading, left Barry 2nd, left Bristol Channel 5th for Western Task Force area (intended for Convoy EBC2Y ETA 8th)

COLWITH FORCE   805/18   Br (West Coast)   left London 6th (but withdrawn from planned Convoy ETC22): returned from beach-head early July

EMPIRE BOSWELL   2,876/42   Br (MoWT) - after loading, left Barry 1st, left Bristol Channel 5th for Western Task Force area (intended for Convoy EBC2Y ETA 8th)

FELSPAR   799/08   Br (Robertson) - arrived London 17th to load, left Thames, ETA Juno 24th (Convoy ETC16)

KYLE BUTE   795/00   Br (Kyle) - after loading, left Cardiff 12th, ETA Utah 16th (Convoy EBC10)

METHILHILL   648/14   Br (Taylor) - after loading, left London 14th, ETA Sword 16th (Convoy ETC10): vessel lost both anchors 27th so returned to Solent

SINCERITY   634/36   Br (Everard) - after loading, left London 14th, ETA Juno 16th (Convoy ETC10)

THE DUKE   820/27   Br (Hay) - ex Humber, left Thames, ETA Eastern Task Force area 18th (Convoy ETC12)

TOLSTA HEAD   673/11   Br (Henry & MacGregor) - after loading, left London 5th, left Thames 0100 7th, ETA Juno 8th (Convoy ETC22): left for London 12th

Section C6 - DEPOT, ACCOMMODATION, CONTROL, (non-assault) HEADQUARTERS AND REPAIR SHIPS, (CRAFT AND BARGES,) DREDGERS, FIREBOATS AND LIGHTSHIPS

These were the naval and merchant ships of a variety of types allocated to static duties off the Normandy coast as well as some of the vessels stationed in UK waters specifically for Neptune operations.

NAME OF VESSEL   Tonnage/year of build, nationality (owner) of merchant ships, type - origin and/or assembly area, destination and convoy: other information. (All dates are June 1944 unless otherwise stated.)

ADONIS   US LST as ARL (repair ship, landing craft) - ex Plymouth, left Weymouth Bay anchorage, arrived Omaha 1224 8th for service at Mulberry A: was in danger of beaching in gale 21st

ADVENTURE   HM minelayer as repair ship - left Solent (Anchorage 22/c8) 2300 7th, arrived Gold 0830 8th (Convoy EWP1) for service at Mulberry B: 1810 30th anchored inside Mulberry B

ALBATROSS   HM seaplane carrier as repair ship - left Thames 0600 7th, arrived Sword 8th (Convoy ETM2) for service at Gooseberry 5: damaged by gunfire 0825 23rd and 26th: moved to Gold 29th

AMBITIOUS   1,849/13   Belgian cross-Channel car ferry LONDON-ISTANBUL as HM minesweeper HQ ship - left Solent (Anchorage 30/c2) 1330 9th: arrived in assigned anchorage in Eastern Task Force area 12th

AORANGI   17,491/24   Br (Canadian Australasian) liner as depot ship for tugs - left Liverpool 29th April, arrived Solent (Anchorage 21/a) 5th May and remained until replaced by EMPRESS OF RUSSIA (16,810/13 Br [Canadian Pacific]) in July

AORANGI, bottom right, at her Solent anchorage. [IWM A23720A]

DESPATCH arriving at Gold on 8th June, 1944. [IWM A24354]

ARISTOCRAT 544/35 Br (London & North Eastern Railway) Clyde passenger vessel TALISMAN as HM HQ ship (Mulberry B) until replaced by DESPATCH - left Solent (Anchorage 22/a4), arrived Gold 0830 7th (Convoy EWC1B)

ASCANIUS 10,048/10 Br (Ocean SS) passenger/cargo vessel as depot ship - left Thames 0600 7th, arrived Juno 1022 8th (Convoy ETM2) for service at Gooseberry 4

ATLAS US LST as ARL (repair ship, landing craft) - ex Falmouth, left Plymouth 7th, arrived Utah for service at Gooseberry 1

BACHAQUERO see Section A4

BEN TARBERT HM depot trawler - left Solent, ETA Omaha 11th (Convoy EBC5W)

BERNARD CARTER 7,191/42 US Liberty type as depot ship - left Barry 5th, left Bristol Channel 1130 5th, arrived Western Task Force area 0800 7th (Convoy EBM2)

CALSHOT 679/30 Br (Southampton Isle of Wight) tender as landing craft engineering and maintenance vessel in Solent area (Force J)

CAP TOURANE 8,009/23 Br (MoWT) ex-French (Chargeurs Reunis) passenger vessel as depot ship - left Thames 0600 7th, arrived Sword 8th (Convoy ETM2) for service at Gooseberry 5: damaged by gunfire 22nd and 25th: moved to Gold 29th

CAPETOWN HM cruiser as depot ship - ex Falmouth, via Weymouth Bay, arrived Omaha 0830 7th (Convoy EBP1) for service at Mulberry A

CERES HM cruiser as depot ship - ex Falmouth, via Weymouth Bay, arrived Utah 0830 7th (Convoy EBP1) for service at Gooseberry 1

CHIMO US auxiliary minelayer as minesweeper depot ship - left Plymouth 0900 6th, arrived Utah 0800 7th (Convoy EBM2)

DANAE see Section B2

DESPATCH HM cruiser as HQ, base and AA defence ship (Mulberry B) - left Solent (Anchorage 22/c9) 2310 7th, arrived Gold 0930 8th (Convoy EWP1)

Dredgers assigned included -

D.M. DREDGE No.16, FOULNEY, H. & B. RY. DREDGER No.4, JAMES No.46, JAMES No.67, NUMBER FOUR, No.32, No.36, RAMSGATE, RED NAB, ROSSALL, T.B. TAYLOR, T.C.C. HOPPER No.1, T.I.C. No.18, T.I.C. No.19, TOLVERNE

ELEAZAR WHEELOCK 7,191/42 US Liberty type as accommodation ship - left Barry 5th, left Bristol Channel 1130 5th, arrived Omaha 0800 7th (Convoy EBM2) for service at Mulberry A

Fireboats -

DEW (for Gold)

M.H. STEPHEN (left Solent 1900 5th for Juno [Assault Convoy J15])

FRATTON 757/25 Br (Southern Railway) vessel as HM Bombardon control ship - left Weymouth Bay 4th for Selsey, arrived Gold 7th (Follow-up Convoy L5/ETM1): returned to Portland 21st

FROBISHER see Section B2

GEORGE D. IRVINE HM depot trawler - initially at Solent then left, ETA Sword 23rd (Convoy EWC2B)

GEORGE W. WOODWARD 7,176/43 US Liberty type as depot ship - left Cardiff 5th, via Solent, ETA Gold 8th (Convoy EBM3) for service to personnel manning US landing craft

HASLEMERE 756/25 Br (Southern Railway) vessel as HM Mulberry Control and receiving ship for Bombardons, Phoenix and Whale and as planters and sappers HQ (Mulberry B) - arrived Gold 7th (Follow-up Convoy L5/ETM1)

HAWKINS see Section B2

ISLE OF THANET see Section A1

KELANTAN 1,106/21 Br (Singapore Straits) vessel as depot and repair ship for minesweepers and anti-submarine trawlers - Solent (Anchorage 30/c1 then 29)

KINGSMILL see Section B1

LAGUNA BELLE 617/96 Br (General Steam) excursion vessel - HQ ship (Mulberry Whale sections) at Peel Bank (Isle of Wight)

Lightships -

JUNO ex Thames: positioned 18th

KANSAS ex Thames: positioned 18th

LSE 1 HM US LST as LSE (landing ship, emergency repair) - in reserve at Plymouth until 23rd when sailed for Solent for service in Eastern Task Force area

LSE 2 HM US LST as LSE (landing ship, emergency repair) - ex Solent (Anchorage 20W/2) for Juno

MELVILLE US destroyer tender - ex Weymouth Bay, at Omaha 12th

MIANTONOMAH US minelayer as Task Force HQ ship - ETA Western Task Force area 25th (Convoy ECP15)

MISOA see Section A4

NORTHLAND (intended for Convoy EBC2Y ETA Western Task Force area 8th)

PRESIDENT WARFIELD 4,273/28 US accommodation ship - ordered to leave Bristol Channel 23rd for Plymouth for service at Omaha in July

QUEEN OF KENT 798/16 Br (New Medway) excursion vessel as HM Mulberry accommodation and despatch control ship - at Peel Bank (Isle of Wight) 3rd-15th then Dungeness

QUEEN OF THANET 792/16 Br (New Medway) excursion vessel as HM Mulberry despatch control ship - at Selsey then at Peel Bank (Isle of Wight) from 24th

RAYMONT HM depot trawler

SANDOWN   see Section C1

SCAWFELL   see Section C1

SKIDDAW   483/96   Br (Campbell) excursion vessel BRITANNIA as HM HQ ship, left Dungeness 14th for Peel Bank (Isle of Wight) for service until 24th

SOUTHERN PRINCE   10,917/29   Br (Prince) vessel as HM HQ ship (British assault area) - left Solent (Anchorage 22/a12) 2305 7th, arrived Juno 8th (Convoy EWP1)

SOUTHLAND   (intended for Convoy EBC2Y ETA Western Task Force area 7th)

STAR OF FREEDOM   HM trawler depot ship - initially at Solent then left, ETA Utah 24th (Convoy EBC17W)

TASAJERA   see Section A4

THOMAS B. ROBERTSON   7,176/42   US Liberty type as accommodation ship - left Barry 5th, via Solent, arrived Utah 8th (Convoy EBM3) for service at Gooseberry 1

THOMAS JOHNSON   7,176/42   US Liberty type as depot ship - left Clyde 13th, via Milford Haven, left Portland, ETA Utah 1st July (Convoy ECM19P)

THYSVILLE   8,351/22   Belgian (Maritime Belge) vessel as depot ship - left Thames 0600 7th, arrived Gold 1200 8th (Convoy ETM2) for service at Mulberry B

TYNE   HM depot ship for fleet destroyers and escorts in Solent anchorages 22, 28 and 29 - left Scapa 0742 1st, arrived Solent (Anchorage 22/b14) 0900 5th

WAR WING   HM depot trawler

WAVENEY   see Section B1

Assigned landing craft and barges

LBE (Landing Barge, Emergency Repair) **1-10**, **12-60**

LBK (Landing Barge, Kitchen) **1-10**

LCE (Landing Craft, Emergency Repair) **13**, **15**, **16**, **19**, **23**, **24**

Section C7 - HOSPITAL CARRIERS

The function of these vessels, with their specially adapted landing craft referred to as 'water ambulances', was to transport casualties, usually to Outer Dock, Southampton, for hospitalisation. Five ships were allocated to each Task Force area. Internationally approved hospital vessels sailed independently, theoretically being exempt from attack: those unapproved moved in convoy under escort.

NAME OF VESSEL   Tonnage/year of build, nationality (owner) - origin and/or assembly area and destination of first sailing: other information. (All dates are June 1944 unless otherwise stated.)

BATAVIER II   1,573/20   Dutch passenger/cargo vessel - left Thames 6th, left Solent, ETA Gold 8th (Convoy EWP1)

DINARD   2,313/24   Br (Southern Railway) cross-Channel passenger vessel - after collision damage repairs, left Southampton 1300 1st, left Solent 1310 7th for Juno: 1805 7th extensively damaged forward by mine whilst outside the swept waters, towed to beach-head 7th then the following day to Solent, where anchored 0200 9th, and Southampton where arrived 1600 same day: under repair until mid July

DUKE OF LANCASTER 3,794/28 Br (London Midland & Scottish Railway) cross-Channel passenger vessel - left Milford Haven 0500 6th for Southampton, left Solent 1200 8th, arrived Gold 1800 same day: left 1215 10th with 245 casualties for Portsmouth Harbour where arrived 2220 same day

DUKE OF ROTHESAY 3,804/28 Br (London Midland & Scottish Railway) cross-Channel passenger vessel - left Thames 0030 6th for Southampton, left Solent 1200 8th for Juno

ISLE OF JERSEY 2,143/30 Br (Southern Railway) cross-Channel passenger vessel - arrived Thames 1st, left, arrived Sword 8th: left 9th

LADY CONNAUGHT 3,147/12 Br (British & Irish) cross-Channel passenger vessel - ex Milford Haven, left Solent 1244 7th, at Utah 8th

ST JULIEN after being mine damaged on 7th June, 1944. [Arthur Russell Collection]

NAUSHON 1,978/29 Br (MoWT) - ex Thames: at Omaha 8th

NEW BEDFORD 1,595/28 Br (MoWT) - left Thames 6th, left Solent, arrived Omaha 8th (Convoy EWP1)

PRAGUE 4,220/30 Br (London & North Eastern Railway) cross-Channel passenger vessel - ex Thames, left Solent 1244 7th for Western Task Force area

ST JULIEN 1,952/25 Br (Great Western Railway) cross-Channel passenger vessel - left Milford Haven 6th, left Solent 1334 7th for Eastern Task Force area: 1912 7th massive hole blown in starboard side, keel towards waterline, by mine whilst outside the swept waters: arrived Southampton under tow by tug JAUNTY 1700 8th: after repairs left Solent for Juno 0300 28th

The hospital ships **EL NIL** (7,775/16 Br [MoWT]) and **LLANDOVERY CASTLE** (10,640/25 Br [Union-Castle]) were both ordered on the 19th to sail south from the Clyde to be on stand-by.

'Bar' vessel and boom trawler with 'Bombardons' at Mulberry B on 8th June, 1944.

Section C8 - MOORING LAYERS

Two mooring forces sailed from the Solent on D-Day to lay buoys and moorings (A in the Western Task Force area and B in the Eastern) for the Mulberry and merchant ship anchorages.

NAME OF VESSEL   Tonnage/year of build, nationality (owner) of major merchant ships - origin and/or assembly area, destination and convoy of first sailing: other information. (All dates are June 1944 unless otherwise stated.)

MOORING FORCE A
left Solent (Anchorage 31) 6th, arrived Utah 7th (Convoy EWC1A)

HM Netlayers

BRITTANY   1,445/33   Br (Southern Railway) passenger vessel - allocated to Mooring Forces A and B: laid 13-buoy trot for Bombardons 7th then laid initial Liberty ship moorings

MINSTER   707/24   Br (Southern Railway) cargo vessel - after laying 12 buoys for hauling off at Utah, sunk by mine 1310 8th: submerged to top of deckhouse, the wreckage still being visible 23rd

HM boom defence vessels

BARBAIN, BARCOMBE, BARTHORPE, BARTIZAN, DRAGONET, PLANTAGENET

Trawlers as boom working vessels

CHERWELL, CORONATIA, LAVEROCK (replacing MOUNT ARD)

HM boom carrier as depot ship

FOSS BECK   4,918/30   Br (Foss Beck) vessel

MOORING FORCE B

left Solent (Anchorage 31) 6th, arrived Eastern Task Force area 7th (Convoy EWC1B)

HM Netlayers

ATALANTA 463/06 Br (Blackpool) passenger vessel: laid initial buoy

RINGWOOD 755/26 Br (Southern Railway) cargo vessel

HM boom defence vessels

BARBERRY (delayed undergoing repairs on the Thames until 7th), **BARCOCK**, **BARLOW**, **BARNWELL**, **BAROVA**, **BARRAGE**, **MARTINET** (delayed Rosyth undergoing repairs, en route to Solent 11th), **SONNET**

Trawlers as boom working vessels

ALIDA (replacing UIVER which withdrawn for repairs), **ANDANES** (replacing GEORGE BLIGH), **THEWAY**

HM boom carrier as depot ship (Mulberry B)

FERNMOOR 4,972/36 Br (Runciman) vessel

Other vessels assigned

BARNDALE HM boom defence vessel - under repair: left Bristol Channel, ETA Solent 25th

CAVEROCK 1,332/15 Br (Verano) vessel as HM boom carrier - left Milford Haven 5th, via Falmouth, left Solent for Mulberry B 14th (Convoy EWL8)

KIRRIEMORE 4,970/35 Br (Runciman) vessel as boom carrier - ex Rosyth

LEONIAN 5,424/36 Br (United Africa) vessel as HM boom carrier - loaded at Pembroke, left Falmouth 8th, left for Mulberry with final moorings approx 14th

NORTHLYN trawler as HM boom working vessel - ex Falmouth

SCOMBER trawler as HM boom working vessel (replacing ROULE) - ex Falmouth, left Solent, ETA Mulberry B 5th July (Convoy ETC27W)

SETTSU trawler as HM boom working vessel - ex Falmouth, left Solent, ETA Mulberry B 5th July (Convoy ETC27W)

Section C9 - NAVAL STORE SHIPS

Armament Supply Issuing Ships (ASIS) and Victualling Supply Issuing Ships (VSIS) were used to replenish naval vessels off the Normandy beach-head: others were specifically allocated to service Neptune ships in home waters.

NAME OF VESSEL Tonnage/year of build, nationality (owner) of merchant ships, type - origin and/or assembly area, destination and convoy of first sailing: other information. (All dates are June 1944 unless otherwise stated.)

ARDGANTOCK 842/19 Br (MacCallum) vessel as ASIS - ex London, left Thames 0215 5th, via Solent, ETA Eastern Task Force area 7th (Convoy EWC1B)

AXINITE 724/28 Br (Robertson) vessel as ASIS - ex Thames (intended for Convoy ETC3 ETA 9th): off beach-head 13th

BALTEAKO   1,328/20   Br (Anglo-Latvian) vessel as VSIS (carrying refrigerated provisions and dry stores) - ex Glasgow, arrived Solent 22nd May: left, ETA Juno 29th (Convoy ETC21)

BEDENHAM   Br ASIS - ex Thames, left Solent, ETA Sword 11th (Convoy ETC5W)

CHATTENDEN   320/43   Br VSIS - left Plymouth, ETA Omaha 25th (Convoy EBC20) for Juno

DONAGHMORE   581/25   Br (Kelly) vessel as ASIS - left Bristol Channel 2nd, via Solent, arrived Utah 7th (Convoy EWC1A): returned to Plymouth

EMERALD QUEEN   481/37   Br (British Channel Islands) vessel as ASIS - ex Bristol Channel for Western Task Force area (intended for Convoy EBC3 ETA 9th): returned to Plymouth where arrived 17th: listed as cased petrol coaster 25th

EMPIRE SNOWDROP   399/39   Dutch CARIBE as Br (MoWT) vessel - ex Cardiff, left Plymouth 18th, ETA Omaha 19th (Convoy ECM11) for Eastern Task Force area

FENDRIS   1,018/25   Br (Moss Hutchison) vessel as ASIS for destroyers and coastal craft - left Milford Haven 16th May for Solent

KINTERBURY   Br ASIS - left Solent, ETA Utah 11th (Convoy EBC5W)

NITRO   US ammunition ship - ex Clyde, arrived Plymouth: re-ammunitioned battleship NEVADA 9th

PROCRIS   1,060/24   Br (Moss Hutchison) vessel as ASIS for destroyers and coastal craft - left Workington 10th May, arrived Solent (Anchorage 25/9) 14th May

RIBBLEBANK   351/21   Br (Ribble) vessel as VSIS - left Plymouth, ETA Omaha 25th (Convoy EBC20) for Juno

ROBERT DUNDAS   Br - left Plymouth, ETA Omaha 13th (Convoy ECM5): first arrival Eastern Task Force area 24th

Section C10 - 'PLUTO' VESSELS

Vessels involved with 'PLUTO' (Pipe Line Under The Ocean) made preparations during June so that fuel pipelines could later be laid across the Channel to Cherbourg and to Boulogne. In the meantime, facilities were provided off the beach-heads to enable tankers to discharge their cargoes by pipeline to the shore.

NAME OF VESSEL   Tonnage/year of build, nationality (owner) of merchant ships, type - origin and/or assembly area, destination of first sailing: other information. (All dates are June 1944 unless otherwise stated.)

ALGERIAN   2,315/24   Br (Ellerman) vessel as HM cable ship - ordered to leave Thames for Southampton end June

HOLDFAST   1,499/21   Br (Dundee, Perth & London) vessel LONDON as HM cable store ship - left Falmouth for Solent 23rd

LATIMER   6,987/41   Br (MoWT) vessel EMPIRE RIDLEY as HM cable ship - left Bristol Channel for Southampton 29th

PERSEPHONE   HM hopper barge W.24 as cable ship - ex Tilbury

SANCROFT [IWM A28822Z]

SANCROFT   6,978/41   Br (MoWT) vessel EMPIRE BAFFIN as HM cable ship - ex Tilbury

Trawlers

CEDAR (carried 'PLUTO' reconnaissance party to beach-head), **GRAMPIAN** (arrived Port en Bessin 16th), **LILAC**

Cable Barges for completing the shore ends

BRITANNIC, GOLDBELL, GOLDDRIFT, OCEANIC, RUNIC

Accommodation Barges for shore end working parties

AETON, GLENMORISTON, LAWSON, NYCTEA

Steel Drums, each with 70 miles of pipe

CONUNS I-VI

Tugs for towing CONUNS. (First tow arrived Southampton 30th from Thames using all three tugs)

BUSTLER, DANUBE V, MARAUDER

Section C11 - PUMPING VESSELS

Mulberry 'Phoenix' sections were 200ft long concrete caissons, for use as breakwaters. They had been flooded down for concealed storage at Selsey and Dungeness and, when required for use off the French coast, had to be pumped out, raised off the sea bed and manoeuvred in preparation for cross-Channel towage. (All dates are June 1944 unless otherwise stated.)

BARENDSZ Dutch schuyt (sent to Dungeness 16th: at Selsey 23rd), **DAPPER** (sent to Dungeness 16th), **DORIA** tug (at Dungeness 25th), **EMPIRE DEMON** tug (at Dungeness 25th), **KING LEAR** (sent to Dungeness 16th), **LAMB** (at Selsey 23rd), **LONGTOW** (at Dungeness 25th), **MIES** Dutch schuyt (at Dungeness 25th equipped with 6" naval salvage pumps), **NOORD-STAD** Dutch schuyt (sent to Dungeness 16th equipped with 6" naval salvage pumps), **RICHARD II** tug (at Dungeness 25th), **ROEBUCK** (left Falmouth 0200 13th for Selsey as accommodation vessel: no longer required 30th), **ROSEDENE** (at Dungeness 25th), **SAMBUR** (left Cardiff 25th May: at Dungeness as accommodation and store ship 25th), **SWIFT** (at Dungeness 23rd), **THAMES COAST** (at Dungeness 23rd), **TORDENSKJOLD** (at Dungeness as accommodation vessel), **URMAJO** (at Dungeness as store ship), **VIDA** Dutch schuyt (sent to Dungeness 16th, at Selsey 23rd), **WATERCOCK** tug (at Dungeness 25th), **YEWDALE** collier (at Dungeness 25th), **ZEEHOND** (at Dungeness 25th), **ZEUS** (under repair Dover: at Dungeness early July)

See also Section C12

Section C12 - SALVAGE VESSELS

These vessels were allocated for salvage duty: the list shows their location in mid May, where known, and any movements noted, all of which are June 1944 unless otherwise stated.

ABIGAIL (Leith: left Portland for beach-head 29th), **ALITA** store carrier (Southampton), **AMERICAN SALVOR** (Plymouth), **BERTHA** (Southampton: at Selsey on Mulberry pumping operations: left for Mulberry B ETA 4th July), **BRANT** (ex Falmouth), **CARMENITA** (Southampton), **DIVER** (ex Plymouth: sent to assist BLACKWOOD 16th), **DORITA** (Southampton), **FORDE** (left Swansea 18th May: at Dungeness as accommodation vessel for Mulberry pumping operations 25th), **FOREMOST 17** (Hartlepool), **FOREMOST 18** (Harwich: left Solent, ETA Eastern Task Force area 8th [Convoy ETC22W]), **GALLIONS REACH** (Immingham: left Thames for beach-head 10th [Convoy ETC5]), **HELP** (Southampton: left Portland for beach-head 29th), **LADY SOUTHBOROUGH** (Southampton: sent to Dungeness on Mulberry pumping operations 16th: under repair 30th), **LE LUTTEUR** (Southampton: at Dungeness on Mulberry pumping operations 23rd), **LIFELINE** (Southampton), **LINCOLN SALVOR** (Southampton), **ML 253** motor launch, **MISS ELAINE** (Portland: sent to assist BLACKWOOD 15th but turned back because of bad weather), **PALMSTON** salvage store carrier (Southampton: left Solent, ETA Eastern Task Force area 30th [Convoy ETC22W]), **POLITA** (Southampton), **SALVAGE CHIEFTAIN** (Swansea: sent from Solent to assist BLACKWOOD 15th but turned back because of bad weather: stood by H.G. BLASDEL 29th), **SALVEDA** (Liverpool), **SALVICTOR** (Southampton: grounded at Mulberry B 16th: towed GLAISDALE 23rd: assisted DERRYCUNIHY 24th), **SEA SALVOR** (Plymouth: left Solent, ETA Eastern Task Force area 8th [Convoy ETC22W: assisted KYLEGORM 22nd), **SOUTHAMPTON SALVOR** (Southampton: arrived Plymouth 30th May), **SUCCOUR** (Blyth: left Thames for beach-head 10th [Convoy ETC5]), **SWIVEL** (ex Plymouth), **UPLIFTER** (Harwich: arrived Thames 20th May), **WHITSTABLE** (assigned 5th to carry US salvage equipment and personnel: left Clyde 6th)

Section C13 - TANKERS

A photograph, dated June 1944, showing a tanker steaming through the Solent, north of Cowes, with MONOWAI and BRIGADIER at anchor (top right). [IWM]

BRITISH STATESMAN [NMM P21677]

NAME OF VESSEL   Tonnage/year of build, nationality (owner) - origin and/or assembly area, destination and convoy of first sailing: other information. (All dates are June 1944 unless otherwise stated.)

BEN ROBINSON   290/23   Br (National Benzole) vessel as water carrier - after loading, left London 4th (intended for Convoy ETC2Y ETA 7th): alongside DESPATCH at Juno 14th

BRITISH ENGINEER   6,993/22   Br (British Tanker) - after loading, left Barry 0830 10th, ETA Omaha 13th (Convoy EBC7) to discharge 9,000 tons petrol and diesel: 2150 12th struck mine amidships on starboard side, vessel diverted to Solent where anchored 0700 13th to transfer part cargo to ROUSEVILLE: left Solent 18th, arrived Thames Haven 20th to discharge remaining cargo

BRITISH PRINCESS   7,019/17   Br (British Tanker) vessel as water carrier - for Eastern Task Force area (intended for Convoy ETC3 ETA 9th): returned 17th

BRITISH RENOWN   6,997/28   Br (British Tanker) - left Solent, ETA Utah 25th (Convoy EBC20W)

BRITISH STATESMAN   6,991/23   Br (British Tanker) vessel as water carrier - left London 30th May, left Thames, ETA Omaha 12th (Convoy ETM6): returned to Solent: on a subsequent voyage, water found contaminated by petrol 24th

CHANT   400/44   Br (MoWT) (showing location [in brackets] on 22nd May and subsequent information on vessels reported at the beach-head during June)

2 -   [Southampton] ETA Sword 14th (Convoy ETC8)

3 -   [Portsmouth] ETA Port en Bessin 23rd (Convoy ETC15)

4 -   [Portsmouth] ETA Eastern Task Force area 25th (Convoy ETC17)

6 - (intended for Convoy ETC2Y ETA 7th)

7 - ETA Juno 11th (Convoy ETC5): driven ashore in gale and capsized at beach-head 19th

22 - [Southampton] (listed as water carrier) ETA Eastern Task Force area 8th (Convoy ETC22)

23 - [Hull] beached in gale 20th: arrived Sheerness under tow 3rd July

25 - ETA Eastern Task Force area 27th (Convoy ETC19)

26 - (intended for Convoy ETC2Y ETA 7th) driven ashore in gale 20th

42 - [Middlesbrough, building] left Middlesbrough 9th, ETA Eastern Task Force area 27th (Convoy ETC19)

50 - [Goole] ETA Eastern Task Force area 27th (Convoy ETC19)

52 - [Dartmouth] at Juno 18th: returned to Hamble 30th

57 - [Portsmouth] ETA Port en Bessin 23rd (Convoy ETC15)

58 - [Portsmouth] ETA Eastern Task Force area 25th (Convoy ETC17): damaged at Port en Bessin 28th: arrived Thames 3rd July

60 - ETA Juno 14th (Convoy ETC8)

61 - (intended for Convoy ETC2Y ETA 7th) capsized at anchor 1345 8th

62 - [Burntisland] ETA Eastern Task Force area 27th (Convoy ETC19)

64 - [Middlesbrough, building] ETA Port en Bessin 23rd (Convoy ETC15)

67 - (intended for Convoy ETC2Y ETA 7th) at Juno 30th

69 - [Portsmouth] ex London, ETA Sword 8th (Convoy ETC22): sank in Juno area 0700 14th carrying 460 tons fresh water from Gold to Sword

DOLABELLA 8,142/39 Br (Anglo-Saxon) vessel as water carrier - left Bristol Channel 6th for Omaha (intended for Convoy EBC3 ETA 9th): returned to Solent 18th

EMPIRE ALDERNEY 288/44 Br (MoWT) vessel as water carrier - ex Hull where delayed for heavy weather damage repairs, left Thames, ETA Juno 12th (Convoy ETC6)

EMPIRE AUDREY 656/43 Br (MoWT) - left London 1st, left Thames 0100 7th, ETA Omaha 8th (Convoy ETC22)

EMPIRE CADET 813/42 Br (MoWT) - left Avonmouth 7th, via Solent, for Juno: returned to Solent 14th

EMPIRE COAST 299/43 Br (MoWT) vessel as water carrier - left London 4th, left Thames, ETA Utah 8th (Convoy ETC22)

EMPIRE CRICKETER 299/44 Br (MoWT) vessel as water carrier - arrived London (Deptford) 27th May, delayed 4 days by stern tube trouble, left Thames, ETA Sword 13th (Convoy ETC7)

EMPIRE DWELLER 667/42 Br (MoWT) - left London 2nd, left Thames 0100 7th, via Solent, for beach-head

EMPIRE GYPSY 813/42 Br (MoWT) - ex Cardiff, left Solent, ETA Juno 1st July (Convoy ETC23W)

EMPIRE HOMESTEAD 296/43 Br (MoWT) vessel as water carrier - left Thames 5th (intended for Convoy ETC2Y ETA 7th)

EMPIRE SETTLER 797/43 Br (MoWT) - anchored Thames 7th, left, ETA Juno 13th (Convoy ETC7)

EMPIRE TROTWOOD 797/44 Br (MoWT) - left Hull 2nd, anchored Thames 3rd, left, ETA Juno 13th (Convoy ETC7): oil contaminated so vessel returned 15th

EMPIRE WRESTLER 797/43 Br (MoWT) - arrived London 24th May, left Thames, ETA Juno 13th (Convoy ETC7)

GOLD SHELL 8,208/31 Br (Anglo-Saxon) vessel (listed as water carrier) - left Falmouth, ETA Gold 15th (Convoy ECM7)

JULIANA   2,587/28   Dutch - left Solent, ETA Juno 23rd/24th (Convoy EWL15)

LOMA NOVIA   1,100/43   Br (MoWT) US - left Solent, ETA Port en Bessin 3rd July (Convoy ETC25W)

LUCITA   2,604/26   Dutch - ex Ipswich, left Thames, ETA beach-head 27th (Convoy ETC19)

LULING   1,164/43   Br (MoWT) US - left Solent, ETA Juno 15th (Convoy ETC9W)

PASS OF BALLATER   796/28   Br (Bulk Oil) - ex Sheerness, left Thames, ETA Juno 11th (Convoy ETC5): returned to Solent 14th

RAPIDOL   2,648/17   Br (Admiralty) - left Solent, ETA Juno 12th (Convoy ETM6W)

RIO BRAVO   1,141/43   Br (MoWT) US - left Solent, ETA Port en Bessin 1st July (Convoy ETC23W)

ROUSEVILLE   1,155/43   Br (MoWT) US - ETA Port en Bessin 29th (Convoy ETC21)

SALT FLAT   1,164/43   Br (MoWT) US - arrived London 26th May (intended for Convoy ETC3 ETA Eastern Task Force area 9th): returned 18th

SAN UBALDO   5,999/21   Br (Eagle Oil) - ex Clyde, left Solent, ETA Juno 24th (Convoy ETC16W) to discharge 6,000 tons furnace oil

SAXET   1,168/43   Br (MoWT) US - left Solent, ETA Port en Bessin 30th (Convoy ETC22W)

WALNUT BEND   1,124/43   Br (MoWT) US - left Hull 26th May, left Thames, ETA Juno 10th (Convoy ETC4)

Y23 -   ex Avonmouth: left Bristol Channel 5th, ETA Omaha 8th (Convoy EBC2Z)

Y25 -   ex Avonmouth: left Bristol Channel 5th, ETA Utah 8th (Convoy EBC2Z)

Y26 -   ex Avonmouth: left Bristol Channel 5th, ETA Utah 8th (Convoy EBC2Z)

Y40 -   ex Swansea: left Bristol Channel 5th, ETA Omaha 8th (Convoy EBC2Z)

Y41 -   ex Swansea: left Bristol Channel 5th, ETA Omaha 8th (Convoy EBC2Z)

Other tankers assigned

BRITISH SCOUT	1,507/22	Br (British Tanker)
CHANT 1, 24, 43, 55, 59	400/44	Br (MoWT)
DARST CREEK	1,135/44	Br (MoWT) US
EMPIRE FLINT	8,129/41	Br(MoWT)
EMPIRE PYM	2,370/44	Br (MoWT)
EMPIRE RUSSELL	3,738/44	Br (MoWT)
EMPIRE TRAVELLER	8,201/43	Br (MoWT)
GOLDEN MEADOW	1,184/43	Br (MoWT) US
HASTINGS	1,135/44	Br (MoWT)
HEYSER	1,164/43	Br (MoWT) US
JUSTINE C. ALLEN	983/30	Br (MoWT)
SEVEN SISTERS	1,185/43	Br (MoWT) US
SULPHUR BLUFF	1,127/44	Br (MoWT)

Y22, **Y24**, **Y27**, **Y38**, **Y42**

Assigned Oil and Water Barges

LBO (Landing Barge, Oiler) **1**-**61**, **63**, **64**, **66**-**73**, **75**-**90**, **92**, **93**, **95**-**98**

LBW (Landing Barge, Water) **1**-**20**

Section C14 - TRAWLERS FOR FUELLING AND SMOKE-MAKING

(All dates are June 1944 unless otherwise stated.)

Fuelling Trawlers - converted HM magnetic minesweeping trawlers fitted with a 33-ton tank for refuelling diesel-driven landing craft.

ATHENIAN(g), **BEN BREAC**(u), **CEVIC**(o), **CHASSE MARIE**(j), **CLYTHNESS**(o), **CONGRE**(g), **CYELSE**(o), **DAMITO**(s), **EMPYREAN**(s), **FENTONIAN**(o) (damaged propeller in Eastern Task Force area 24th, so towed to Solent by tug KROOMAN), **GAROLA**(j), **GOOSANDER**(u), **KING EMPEROR**(j), **LIBYAN**(j), **LUDA LORD**(o), **MILFORD KING**(g), **MONTANO**(u), **NEW COMET**(g), **ORIZABA**(j), **OUR BAIRNS**(o), **OUTPOST**(o), **QUERCIA**(o), **RAETIA I**(j), **REGARDO**(o) (stranded 21st), **RETURNO**(o), **RONSO**(j), **RUGBY**(g), **SANSON**(j), **SATURN**(u), **SHELDON**(o), **STAR OF BRITAIN**(j), **STRATHCOE**(j), **THE ROMAN**(u), **TOKYO II**(j), **TRANSVAAL**(o), **TRITON**(o), **VIDONIA**(g), **VINDELICIA**(s), **YTHAN BRAES**(g)

Allocated (g) Force G; (j) Force J; (o) Force O; (s) Force S; (u) Force U

Smoke-Making (Esso) Trawlers. The purpose of these vessels was to create defensive smoke screens at each Mulberry harbour. The plan was for 30 trawlers to be allocated to each Mulberry and for 3 trawlers to be held in reserve at Aberdeen. While half were in service, the other 15 from Mulberry A would be at Portland for replenishment and the 15 from Mulberry B would be at Southampton. The groups probably included the following -

GROUP A1   - ex Yarmouth, passed Dungeness 0630 8th, arrived Mulberry A 9th

ADELPHI (formerly SIESTA), **ALL HALLOWS** (formerly JAMAICA), **BEN GLAS**, **BRAES O'MAR**, **CLOUGHSTONE**, **CONTROLLER**, **CREVETTE**, **ETRUSCAN**, **NORDKAPP**, **PITSTRUAN**, **STRATHMARTIN**, **WAR STAR**

GROUP A2   - ex Yarmouth, left Thames 11th for Mulberry A

AMBITION (formerly THRUSH), **ARABESQUE** (formerly YESSO), **AVONDEE**, **BARNSNESS** (rammed a coaster at Omaha 19th), **BENJAMIN COLEMAN**, **EROICAN**, **PEGGY NUTTEN**, **SHIELBURN**

GROUP B1   - ex Dover, left Bracklesham Bay 8th, arrived Mulberry B 9th
KERNEVEL, **TAIPO**, **WILLIAM STROUD**

- left Harwich 2nd, left Solent, ETA Mulberry B 9th
ANN MELVILLE, **BRUINSVISCH**, **CORYPHENE** (formerly SILURIA), **ERIDANUS** (formerly PELICAN), **JACQUELINE CLASINE**, **LEPHRETO**, **PRINCE VICTOR**, **RIVER LEVEN**

- ex Thames, left Bracklesham Bay 8th, ETA Mulberry B 9th
ISABEL, **RIANO**, **SALVINI**, **WITHAM**

GROUP B2   - ex Rosyth, left Thames 10th, left Solent 11th, ETA Mulberry B 12th (Convoy ETC6)

BONA, **BUCEPHALUS** (formerly VENTURE), **CHOICE** (formerly STALKER), **GENERAL BIRDWOOD**, **GOEREE** (formerly DOLFIJN), **HEROINE** (formerly HERO), **MARIA ELIZABETH**, **MARIE JOSE ROSETTE**, **MIRABELLE**, **ROXANO**, **STAUNCH** (formerly BENGAL), **STRATHALLADALE** (anchoring gear declared unsatisfactory 15th), **STRATHFINELLA**, **STURTON**, **TOCSIN** (formerly LIBRA)

Other Smoke-Making Trawlers assigned

BERVIE BRAES, **DANDOLO** (sent to Yarmouth with defective winch 7th), **EAST COAST** (sent to Grimsby with defective winch 7th), **IBIS II**, **MIKASA** (ex Yarmouth, left Thames 17th, left Solent, ETA Utah 20th [Convoy EBC15W]), **MUROTO** (arrived Aberdeen 2nd), **RIGOLETTO**, **RIVER SPEY**, **ST MINVER**, **SOUTHWARD HO** (left Tyne 10th), **UGIEBANK**, **VIKING DEEPS** (at Aberdeen)

Section C15 - TUGS

Tugs handling a Mulberry 'Phoenix'. [IWM BH24844]

Tugs were required for rescue duty; to accompany the blockships, many of which were old or in poor condition; to tow barges and Mulberry sections and to undertake normal harbour duties off the French coast. Listed below are the initial June 1944 assignments of the tugs, as far as is known, together with other information relative to that month.

Rescue Tugs

AMSTERDAM - ex Tilbury: towed H.G. BLASDEL to Solent 29th

ARIKARA - ex Portland: at Omaha 8th: towed LA SURPRISE to Solent 21st

+**ATR 3** - sent to assist USS NELSON 12th

+**ATR 4**

+**ATR 15** - left Solent for beach-head 14th (Convoy EWL8)

BANNOCK - ex Plymouth: towed OSPREY 6th: fouled wreckage 11th

JAUNTY - left Solent for Eastern Task Force area (Follow-up Convoy L1): took in tow a landing craft which sank 6th: towed ST JULIEN to Solent 7th/8th: suffered slight hull damage 18th

KIOWA - ex Plymouth: towed GLENROY 18th

MASTODONTE - ex Solent

PINTO - ex Weymouth Bay: at Omaha 8th

SCHELDE - left Solent for Eastern Task Force area (Follow-up Convoy L1): stood by JAMES A. FARRELL 29th

THAMES - ex Solent: towed SCYLLA to Solent 24th

ZWARTE ZEE - left Solent 7th; towed GLENROY 18th: towed AFD No.50 to Mulberry B 26th and JAMES A. FARRELL to Solent 29th

+ ATR = US Ocean Tug, Rescue

EMPIRE HENCHMAN towing a 'Spud' pierhead off Mulberry B on 14th June, 1944

Assigned to tow Mulberry 'Bombardon' sections

These were 200ft long floating steel tanks, assembled at Portland, for mooring off each Normandy beach-head, to form an outer floating breakwater. The first four tows sailed at 1700 6th from Portland Harbour (eastern side)

ABEILLE No.21* (later towed ULSTER Solent to Cardiff 20th-23rd), **ATTENTIF***, **CHAMPION***, **EMPIRE IVY***, **EMPIRE JESTER**, **EMPIRE MEADOW**, **EMPIRE PIXIE***, **EMPIRE RACE***, **EMPIRE SINEW***, **GOLIATH*** (Dutch crew had been replaced early June following Master's refusal to obey orders), **ST MARTIN** (later assisted BLACKWOOD 16th), **ST MELLONS**

* completed Bombardon duty and arrived Solent 16th

Escorted 'Corncobs' (Blockships)

EMPIRE AID (with Corncob III), **EMPIRE BETSY** (left Portland 6th, rescued disabled barges en route, arrived Mulberry B 1515 7th and remained off beach-head throughout June), **EMPIRE DORIS** (with Corncob III), **EMPIRE HENCHMAN**, **EMPIRE HUMPHREY**, **EMPIRE JOHN** (ex Oban with Corncob III), **EMPIRE JONATHAN** (with Corncob I to Gooseberry 4), **EMPIRE LARCH** (with Corncob I to Gooseberry 4: towed THAMES QUEEN to Solent 24th), **EMPIRE RUPERT** (ex Oban), **EMPIRE WINNIE** (ex Oban with Corncob III, arrived Mulberry B 1515 7th and remained off beach-head throughout June)

Towed battleship COURBET to beach-head

left Weymouth Bay 7th, arrived 8th

GROWLER, SAMSONIA

SAMSONIA in August 1946. [Wright & Logan]

Towed ammunition barges
left Littlehampton 6th, arrived Mulberry B 7th each towing three barges

DANUBE VI, **GOOLE No.10** (allocated to local rescue duty Solent area 10th), **QUEENS CROSS**

Towed 2 pontoons each
left Solent 2100 7th, ETA beach-head 8th (Convoy ETC22W)

CHARING CROSS, **DUNDAS** (later sunk in collision 23rd), **EUSTON CROSS**, **FAIRPLAY ONE**, **KING'S CROSS**, **STOKE**

Towed barges from Cardiff to beach-head
DONAU (left 9th), **EBRO** (delayed by leak until 17th), **HUDSON** (left 2230 7th for Utah), **#LT 156** (left 8th for Omaha), **SEINE**

LT = US Large Tug

US **ST** (Small Tugs)
left Solent in Convoys EWC1A and EWC1B ETA 7th

ST 247, **248**, **758**, **759**, **761**, **762**, **767**, **768**, **769**, **771**

A 'Bombardon' tow arrives off the beach-head on 11th June, 1944. [IWM A23996]

'Phoenix' and 'Whale' tows
Phoenix units were concrete caissons, which had been parked at Selsey and Dungeness, for use as breakwaters off the beach-heads. Whales were the pier sections of the harbours. The smaller sections were towed across the Channel up to six pieces at a time, from Peel Bank (Isle of Wight): nearly a third of these were lost in bad weather during the Channel crossing. The first Whale tows sailed at 0330 8th: the first 'Spud' pierhead left on the 11th. The Phoenix and Whale movement schedule included the use of the following tugs -

ETA BEACH-HEAD 9TH
Phoenix tows to Mulberry A

BODIE ISLAND (on a subsequent crossing, Phoenix tow capsized en route approx 20th), **CHEERLY** (later towed ASA ELDRIDGE to Solent 22nd), **FARALLON** (later towed STELLA RIGEL 29th and towed JOHN A. TREUTLEN to Solent 29th), **RESOLVE**

Phoenix tows to Mulberry B
BANDIT, **TRINIDAD HEAD**

Whale tows to Mulberry A
ALLEGIANCE, **ATR 99**, **CORMORANT** (later assisted SANDOWN 20th)

Whale tows to Mulberry B
EMINENT, **LARIAT** (towed broken down LCT back to Solent 5th), **SABINE**, **SAUCY** (on a subsequent crossing, Whale tow foundered 27th)

ETA 10TH
Phoenix tows to Mulberry A
ALGORMA (tow sank 0125 10th), **KEWAYDIN, MAMMOUTH**

Phoenix tows to Mulberry B
EMPHATIC (later broke down 12th and 20th), **FREEDOM** (later towed GLAISDALE to Immingham 24th-27th), **MOOSE PEAK**

Whale tows to Mulberry A
CONTEST, EMPIRE BASCOBEL, ENVOY (later towed SCYLLA to Solent 24th), **FLAUNT, SEAMAN, SUPERMAN**

Whale tows to Mulberry B
ABEILLE No.20 (under repair at Portland 7th), **BAT, DESTINY, EMPIRE SARA, KROOMAN** (later towed FENTONIAN to Solent 24th), **OWL, PRIZEMAN, STORMKING** (rescued survivors from SESAME 11th)

ETA 11TH
Phoenix tows to Mulberry A and B
BLACK ROCK (later assisted FURY 22nd), **BUCCANEER, GAY HEAD, GREAT ISAAC, GRIPER, SANKATY HEAD**

Whale tows to Mulberry A and B
ASSIDUOUS (fouled wire 7th), **EMPIRE FOLK** (while on ammunitioning duty, towed LCT 413 6th: was first tug to work off beach-head 6th: sent to Selsey 28th), **EMULOUS** (refitting until left Thames 7th), **PARTRIDGE** (towed broken down LCT to Solent 5th: sunk by E-boat torpedo 0215 11th), **SESAME** (hit amidships starboard side and sunk by E-boat torpedo approx 0200 11th)

ETA 12TH
Phoenix tow to Mulberry A
HILLSBORO INLET

KROOMAN with 'Bombardons' in Weymouth Bay in May 1944.

Other tugs assigned

DEXTEROUS

EMPIRE BELLE - towed MONARCH to Portsmouth 14th

EMPIRE BEN - refitting on the Thames until 22nd

EMPIRE ROGER - Whale tow sank at Mulberry B 0300 28th: rescued survivors from MAID OF ORLEANS 28th

EMPIRE SERAPH - on Solent ammunitioning duty until 10th: towed Whale to Mulberry A ETA 19th

EMPIRE SILAS - arrived beach-head 1400 8th: later towed ammunition barges from Solent to Juno

EMPIRE VINCENT - initially on Solent ammunitioning duty (during which damaged propeller 8th) then towed Whale to Mulberry A ETA 13th

LADY BRASSEY - towed LST 981 to Solent 6th and EMPIRE LOUGH to be beached near Dover 24th

LYNCH - on Solent ammunitioning duty until 10th then towed Whale to Mulberry A ETA 13th

SEA GIANT

SEA KING

SOLITAIRE - towed to Omaha by BALSAM 19th but capsized 0745 20th

US **ATA** (ocean tug, auxiliary) **2** (ex Portland), **3** (ex Plymouth), **4** (ex Solent), **13** (ex Plymouth), **15** (ex Solent), **54** (ex Plymouth), **125** (ex Plymouth), **170** (ex Plymouth), **172** (ex Solent: towed GOODSON from Portland to Belfast)

ATR 13, **47**, **54**, **97** (all four towed store barges from Exmouth to Western Task Force area)

LT 2, **4**, **5**, **22**, **23**, **130** (all six towed store barges from Exmouth to Western Task Force area), **152**, **214**, **532**, **533**, **534**, **639**

ST 338, **344**, **760**, **766**, **770**, **773**, **781**, **794**, **795**

14 Army-manned **TID** tugs left for beach-head 14th

'Pluto' tugs see Section C10: Mulberry pumping tugs see Section C11

Section C16 - WRECK DISPERSAL VESSELS

These vessels were assigned to wreck dispersal duties: the following list shows the location of each vessel in mid May and any movements noted, all of which are June 1944 unless otherwise stated.

ADMIRAL SIR JOHN LAWFORD (Penarth, at Plymouth 11th), **ARY** (Sheerness), **BURKE** (Sunderland: ordered to leave Thames for Solent 22nd), **CLYNE CASTLE** (North Shields), **COLCHESTER** (formerly FELIXSTOWE) (Harwich then Chatham), **JACINTA** (Sheerness), **LAUREL** (Port Talbot: ordered to leave Thames for Solent 22nd), **LUNE** (Cardiff), **MADDEN** store carrier (Harwich), **MARIA** (Barry via Plymouth), **ONETOS** store carrier (Sheerness), **RAMPANT** (Grimsby then Chatham: ordered to leave Thames for Solent 22nd), **SUNLIGHT** store carrier (Grimsby: ordered ex Thames to Juno 2nd July), **TEHANA** (Barry then Plymouth), **YEZO** (Sheerness: sent to search for disabled landing craft 8th: left Solent for beach-head 14th [Convoy EWL8])

INDEX OF ALLIED NAMED VESSELS
and of unnamed vessels by type

The figures in italics denote the page numbers of photographs

The US cruiser AUGUSTA in 1943. [NMM N6610]

The infantry landing ship EMPIRE MACE. [NMM P22369]

The Liberty ship EZRA WESTON in November 1943. [NMM P22579]

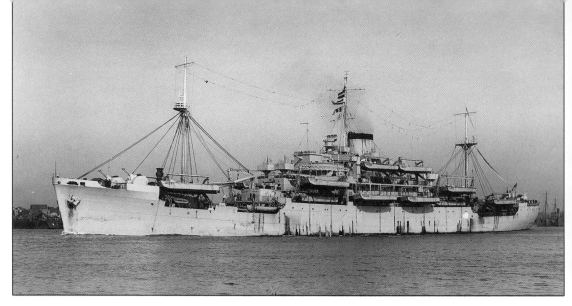

The infantry landing ship GLENROY in May 1946. [Wright & Logan]

The infantry landing ship PAMPAS as PERSIMMON in April 1946. [Wright & Logan]

HM destroyer SERAPIS in December 1943.

The coaster THE PRESIDENT post-war. [A. Duncan]

Printed in Great Britain by MHB Design & Print, Brighton

Aerial view of Mulberry B (Arromanches) Harbour. [IWM MH2407]